RETAIL DETAILED:
SECRETS TO SELLING RETAIL CHAIN STORES

By

Merrill Lehrer

1stBooks - rev. 3/25/02

ACKNOWLEDGEMENTS

This book is dedicated to Betsy and Adam Lehrer for steadfastly believing in me and enduring countless hours of my rants about business, retail stores and the elements of buying merchandise.

Also, I offer deep thanks to Bill Miller, a sixty-something-year-old samurai sales warrior, U.S. Marine, educator and friend.

I am indebted to my mother, Laurel Lehrer, for imparting the wisdom and patience of a saint.

Finally, this book wouldn't have been realized without years of training provided by the master editor, writer and tenacious businessman, Stanley Lehrer, my father.

Table of Contents

PREFACE

SALESPEOPLE: I want you to sell more merchandise, more successfully, to more retail chain store buyers. I want you to avoid all the pitfalls of the numerous sales warriors who have called on me over the years.

Who am I? I am the retail samurai merchant. Perhaps I was the buyer or merchandise manager sitting across the desk from some of you. Those who were prepared flourished in their dealings with me. Others were not so fortunate. Retailing is a tough profession, with innumerable hours spent pouring over sales information, searching for details to drive businesses. Retail is detail. If you weren't meticulous, I, the buyer, wasn't that pleasant. I have crushed a few peddlers along the way. However, many well-organized salespeople were very successful with me.

I've been an assistant buyer, buyer, senior buyer and merchandise manager for the top specialty, department and super stores in America, in a career that has spanned more than 25 years. I've played the game with really terrific sales people, dominating huge multi-million dollar businesses, and negotiating rather gigantic deals. But I played the game with my cards pretty close to the vest. There was no way that I would have shown you my hand. I wouldn't tell you my plan or what was going on in my cranium. Back then, I was on the retailer's payroll.

In this book, I'm putting the cards on the table face up. I'm revealing buying skills that are utilized on a daily basis in the retail world. Why am I doing this? I want to help you and many other salespeople and manufacturers to be more successful in your dealings with retail stores. There is way too much miscommunication in business today. If I can cut through the haze for you and reveal the inner thoughts of the retail buyers, you should be able to understand how they conduct themselves. Speak their language, improve the communication and your business with them should prosper. That is my goal.

I also want to provide this book as a guide for existing retail buyers. Although it's a charming way to learn a career, most buyers are taught their craft through trial and error, without textbooks. Retail buyers operate in an almost mysterious fashion, but it's not rocket science. The buying profession is a covert society that delights in passing their methodology out via verbal means. It's time to deliver the secrets in a more professional manner.

I'd like this book to guide your sales careers. I also want the retail business to boom. If I can show you a different path—one filled with wisdom, logic and preparation—your livelihood should undergo a change. I'd like to lead you down the road to a special place. When you get there, you will be armed for the challenge, prepared to confront the retail store buyer.

Are you ready? It's time for your metamorphosis. It's time for you to become a retail samurai salesperson.

Introduction

Everyone lives by selling something.

Robert Louis Stevenson
Author

In the olden days, sellers sold and buyers bought. They were magical times. The history of retail sales is filled with stories of street merchants lining foreign thoroughfares, little ramshackle booths and peddlers hawking products near ports of call. The wild, uncharted western United States had its weather-beaten, rickety, slat board stores on the frontier, trading posts where pioneers pushing across America bartered for needed wares. As a retailer, once you owned the goods back then, you were totally responsible for the success or failure of the product and its sales rate. Customer service and an exchange policy didn't exist. The manufacturer didn't service your account. But that was a long time ago.

The retail world today has a distinctly different landscape. Salespeople don't merely hand off the merchandise to a store and collect a check for the goods. The salesperson's life is infinitely more complicated than that. Nowadays, the seller's responsibilities go way beyond the initial sale. Corporate retail store buyers have expectations that must be met if a salesperson is to be successful. If the seller doesn't meet the buyer's needs, it's unlikely that the store will purchase products in the future from that source.

A salesperson representing a manufacturer must take care of their customer, the retail store buyer. Today, a salesperson must convince the retail store buyer to first buy the goods. Then, the salesperson must monitor how the products sell after the purchase and provide sales support at store level. Also, the salesperson must offer point of purchase signing, redesign packaging, and provide markdown allowances and coop advertising programs. If the merchandise doesn't fly out the door, the salesperson must take back things that don't sell and damages. Salespeople also will encounter poorly trained buyers and they must learn the art of covering the ass of the buyer when they make mistakes. You can meet with the buyer, giving them a product and proposal exactly as they've requested, and then you won't get a response. Phone calls placed to the buyer won't be returned. There's the regular turn over of personnel in the buying office and on the sales floor, so salespeople are always training someone new. Whew!! Its enough responsibility to give you heart palpitations.

If you're a salesperson and you're calling on a buyer or a corporate retail headquarters, all of the above shouldn't be new to you. As if that isn't enough to make you scream out of your office window, other people are conspiring against you. While you are dealing with the intricate needs of the buying office, your competition is waging a guerrilla war against you, taking store managers and buyers out to lunch to get information about you and your products. Ethics are non-existent to these people. Some of them will tell the buyer tall tales about your products and why their goods are superior. It's not uncommon for one vendor to offer to buy out another manufacturer's items on the shelf, making room for their products. Some suppliers will do anything to get an advantage over you. Buyers love this— they're more than happy to play one supplier against another—and they will win no matter what happens.

Meanwhile, bombs are going off in buyer's offices. They are disorganized and slammed by the workload and have limited, untrained bodies to help them to do the job. As a salesperson, you desperately need the buyer to move the process along, to decide to buy your product, to enter the merchandise specifications into their computer system, and to eventually generate a purchase order. But it's not that simple.

Buyers today are focussed on way too many things. Years ago, they were responsible for picking merchandise, running ads and negotiating deals with suppliers. Today is different. Big business stretches buyers to the breaking point, requiring many to work nights and weekends to keep up with the pace. How are you going to get the buyer to purchase your items? Many of them don't even have time to eat lunch sometimes.

How can you help the buyer? How can you be more successful with them? If you understand the buyer—how they evaluate their business, how they will perceive you, what is affecting their daily schedule—you just might sell them your merchandise.

You sell products for a living to retail store buyers. I'm sure that many of you are great salespeople. You've probably taken a few courses along the way that taught you how to further hone your skills.

But I'm not here to teach you how to sell. I'm here to arm you with information about your customer, the retail buyer, information they probably don't want you to know. When you understand exactly how a buyer thinks, how they're judged by their company, and the rules they play by, you will have an improved relationship with them. Master the way they think, and you should be able to land more product in their stores. But if you approach the buyer like just another salesperson, the buyer will probably blow you off.

You sell for a living and you're good at that. But you're sitting across the desk from your nemesis, the gatekeeper—the person who holds the pencil that writes the orders. They have power in that pencil. The buyer can order your goods and make you successful in your business, or they will pass you by and give business to your competition. It's your choice.

Take all the sales courses you want, but they won't let you into the mind of the buyer. Now, I know, getting inside a buyer's mind is a very scary place. Some of you might think that visiting the inside of a buyer's brain must be a lot like visiting a psycho ward in a mental institution.

Do you know what? You're not wrong. How do I know? Because I was a buyer, and a divisional merchandise manager and a vice president of merchandising. I was the beast who sat across the desk from scores of great sales people. Many products never crossed the threshold and never entered my assortment. However, some vendors did get me excited about their goods when they approached me in an intelligent fashion—they understood my needs, and I rewarded them with my business.

Do you think you know all these principles? Do you? Well, I certainly hope that you're reading this because you want to learn how a buyer thinks. Although the computer has impacted retail and more data is available to analyze products today vs. 25 years ago, buying principles have not changed. I'm happy to share them with you. Armed with this information, you will be light years ahead of your competition and you're likely to approach the buyer with greater skill and understanding of their needs. Approach the buyer the right way and you're likely to sell them merchandise.

Years ago, I received one of the best compliments during my 25 year career. I was a buyer at the headquarters for a little office supply chain down in Florida, I think it was called Office Depot. One supplier had magically connected to my needs. Together, we improved packaging and introduced brand new products—we set the standard in the industry. This supplier's executive vice president, a gentleman named Andy Roth, understood the retail buyer and was able to consistently give me what I required to be successful. One day, he complimented me. Andy and I had revolutionized a basic, core business together—file folders. Trust me, no product is more basic, or mundane, than file folders. Despite that, we energized the category. Resulting sales for my company were off the charts, and my new products were light years ahead of my competition's offerings.

Do you know what Andy said to me? I had fought till the death for my company, upholding the highest standards, and my sales showed it. I successfully differentiated my store from many others. Andy said, "Merrill, you are a retail samurai warrior."

But this executive vice president was only half correct. He was a samurai too. He had mastered the way buyers thought, and he had consistently given me what I needed to succeed.

You can be samurai sales warriors too. Although I am an intelligent man, I am not a rocket scientist. You don't need to be a rocket scientist either to master these concepts.

I was taught buying principles in classrooms at one company, but I largely learned how to buy OTJ—on the job.

What am I going to do? I'm going to tell you these principles, these secrets, the way the buyer thinks. Buyers today don't have the time for teaching you what they want and need for their stores. Their goal is increased sales and if you impede the process, or require too much handholding, you won't be doing business with that buyer forever.

You know what I used to do as a buyer when I'd encounter a vendor who couldn't make me look good to my corporation? Where did a vendor go when they didn't understand what my company needed from a supplier? It might take a year or two, but I would make a change and eliminate that vendor.

Folks who understood my language would get lots more business. I'd transfer business to them from weaker vendors.

You're reading this because you want to be more successful salespeople. You're here because you deal with buyers, store owners, or folks who make the buying/purchasing decision. Let me help you to improve your approach with these gatekeepers. Let me show you their thought processes and their rules.

C'mon. Let's take a walk on the wild side. Let's take you deep inside the cranium, the head, of a retail buyer.

Chapter 1

Think Like A Merchant

The right merchant is one who has the just average of faculties we call common sense; a man of a strong affinity for facts, who makes up his decision on what he has seen. He is thoroughly persuaded of the truths of arithmetic.

Ralph Waldo Emerson
"Wealth," The Conduct of Life (1860)

The salespeople sat across from me on a sofa. We'd looked for an empty meeting room to crash at the Marriott, but nothing was available. So, here we were, discussing our annual financial agreement, right out in the open spaces of a hotel lounge, with a coffee table in between us. Both men were major executives of their corporation, certainly earning well over $100,000 each. You'd never suspect that they represented a multi-million dollar vendor for my store, or that they were proposing the richest financial incentive package ever.

Once a year, in many retail stores in America, it is customary to meet with your suppliers and negotiate a big bucks deal. You've heard the terms before—rebate, incentive plan, program, financial package, and others. Typically, the customer (retailer) and supplier work out an arrangement that challenges and rewards the customer for growing the business.

So, on this November day, I sat in a lounge gazing out the hotel window at the palm trees swaying in the breeze, near Ft. Lauderdale, Florida. The tranquility outside contrasted sharply with the tension around the table. My supplier desperately needed my business; I was his second biggest customer, soon to be number one. He and his boss couldn't afford to displease me. My company's sales were taking off like a rocket, and this vice president of sales and his boss were strapped inside the capsule, going for the ride of their lives.

I remember that the vice president handed me a perfectly rich financial deal in writing, filled with monetary inducements for hitting various purchase plateaus. For example, some financial packages might offer a 1% rebate if you purchased $1,000,000 of goods—a pretty healthy bit of encouragement. This vice president had worked very hard to create this deal, and he and his boss sitting next to him seemed worn out from the process. They alluded to internal arguments over such a huge payout. The rebate program was multi-tiered, offering cash back for 4 different purchase levels.

He had put his cards on the table and, if you believed what he said, he had given me the best deal his company had ever offered to a customer.

My cards were hidden. Many thoughts were coursing through my brain. It was a good deal—in fact, it was the best deal this vendor had ever offered to me. Although this manufacturer had been in business for over 100 years, the VP of sales and his boss were still babes in the woods to me. They'd only dealt with the likes of me for the past year, and they came from a kinder and gentler age. Everything was in slow motion. Their facial expressions were taunt and waiting for me to make my move, and some degree of fear was in their eyes because I hadn't leapt forward, thanking them profusely for their offer.

I had received a different monetary deal a few weeks earlier from their competition. But their competition couldn't service the full United States, and I did need them to fill the void. Also, their competition didn't always subscribe to the work ethic and I repeatedly had stock problems. The vice president sitting on the sofa represented an old style manufacturer, but they always delivered on time and with all items ordered.

In retrospect, this financial package in front of me needed to be evaluated side by side with the competitive offer. Typically, there were many similarities. But I didn't have time for all that back then. My company had raised my sales and profit goals, making them barely achievable. The only way I was going to hit my plan was with major incentives—lots of rebate checks. But the vendor across from me didn't know that. They also hadn't talked to enough people about my style, what kind of buyer I was. They didn't know that I wasn't a nice guy.

"So, Merrill, what do you think? We've really stepped up to the plate, haven't we," the VP asked.

I paused to heighten the effect, leaned forward in my seat, lifted my head gradually, aiming my eyes like lasers targeted at their heads, boring holes deep into their brains.

"Well, I was hoping for more, so much more," I replied. "In fact, I have to tell you, this misses the mark by a long shot. Really, really, way off. I'm very surprised by what you're offering me here. Why, this puts you in a rather precarious position."

"Merrill, I...," the vice president was stammering. He and his boss were shocked.

"Please. Let me finish. You came all this way and you offer me this. Is my business important to you? Because if it is, why would you offer me something like this? I'm very surprised by this and, frankly, I'm going to have to re-evaluate our entire relationship based on this."

In slow motion, with every nano-second feeling like 10 years, I saw the vice president of sales for this major manufacturer fall backwards into his seat, his back sinking deeply into the cushions on the couch. If a wall had been behind him, he would have broken through it. His countenance rapidly changed, going from stages of disbelief, to worry and fear, and finally settled on humiliation. He was beaten, shattered, and unable to speak. I watched as the color left his face and he was ashen, dazed, and I remember thinking that he was dying right in front of me. He had turned a much whiter shade of pale. It looked like he was having a stroke.

I had strong-armed him and, one week later, he caved in to my demands. I picked up several percentage points more in rebate, and his deal did beat his competition.

Now, years later, I'm not too proud of my performance that day and, hopefully, this supplier forgot about this incident long ago. You see, I really didn't negotiate with the man, I merely forced him to offer more. There was no give and take; there was no reason involved. He wasn't prepared for me and he suffered as a result. If he had truly understood the buyer and was prepared, he might have had a chance.

Why are you reading this? Because you want to be prepared. Salespeople typically take more classes and read numerous books on the art of the sale. Buyers and their assistants normally receive very little structured training. The better prepared you are for the buyer, the higher the likelihood of you completing your objectives. You'll have the edge. But there's another reason that you're reading this book. Pain—you want to avoid pain. It's painful to miss business. Are you truly getting enough business? You don't want to be in a painful situation when you're facing down a retail chain store buyer.

Why else are you reading this? Pleasure. The better you understand the buyer, the more business you are likely to get. That could mean more money, and money is wonderfully tied to pleasure.

THOUGHT #1

Think Like a Merchant or Forever Act Like a Peddler

One of my best suppliers in the past decade made the statement above. I had interacted with Larry Cobb many times and each session was the same. He listened, he responded, and he often delivered exactly what I needed. His attitude was always superb. I enjoyed working with him—and his stuff sold.

"Larry, how is it that you consistently give me exactly what I need?" I asked him.

"Well, I never forget to think from the perspective of the retailer. You know, here are your choices: you can think like a merchant or you'll forever act like a peddler."

Larry's words conjured up a vision of two people: one, a successful merchant businessperson sitting in an office and, the other, a street salesman trying to sell pencils out of a cup on a sidewalk. Larry chose to delve into the buyer's psyche, thinking like a great merchant, and he hit homeruns more often than other salespeople. Together, we repackaged mundane products, built upscale merchandise, and filled niches in my store.

Think like a merchant, or forever act like a peddler. What a brilliant thought. Put yourself into the buyer's mind, or forever you will be relegated to a mediocre sales existence. A salesperson should never aspire to mediocrity.

I've met other salespeople like Larry during my lifetime, folks who listened, examined my needs, cut through old beliefs with a Samurai sword, handing me win after win. They "thought out of the box," and didn't let paradigms rule their minds. Listen to the customer, or give the buyer what they want.

I have been fortunate to find exemplary salespeople everywhere I've worked. Most salespeople have an agenda and they stick to it. Others are like the old style traveling salesman. They enter the buyer's office with a ring binder lined with index tabs and they slowly go through their presentation point by boring point. The smart salespeople did have presentations, but these were created after much research into my needs. They'd talk with me and ask great questions. See, buyers love to talk; big egos seem to go with the job requirements. All they had to do was ask me, and I'd spill my guts.

Later in life, as businesses grew larger, I didn't have as much time. If a salesperson didn't delve into my business through other means—researching the industry, their competition, my competition, market prices and more—I didn't have the time to teach them. This separated the pros from the weekend warriors. The best salespeople today come to a meeting armed with information. The worst salespeople offer to give you whatever you need, but they don't have a clue. Today, great salespeople have fully formulated concepts and products to present. Nimrods have half-baked ideas and ask for your help in fleshing them out. Sorry, but I don't have the time. Have a nice day, you turkey, and thanks for wasting my time.

Now, ask yourselves this: Are you a sales warrior or do you just drag product from office to office. Is there a greater purpose to your movements? Do you communicate that to the buyer?

I believe that you're reading this book because you're good at selling, and you'd like to improve your skills. Connect with the buyer, and you just could make more money. But look at the buyer closely. Are they your business partner? Or are you just trying to cram goods into their store?

4

The Gatekeeper

When you enter the buyer's inner sanctum, you are sitting across the desk from "the gatekeeper." That's right, they guard the gate. It's their job to open and close the gate depending on who is on the other side. They negotiate the deals. Show them that you're their friend and can help them to achieve their financial objectives and they might open the door and let you in. However, if you try to impress them with a lukewarm concept, or if you show them something that doesn't vaguely resemble anything they might ever carry in their assortment, lights out. Bye-bye and good night. They don't have time for this.

The buyer has "the power of the pencil." All right, I know that it's an old expression, meaning that the buyer's signature used to appear on purchase orders (PO). For all the big chains in America, buyers don't sign the PO's any more—they're generated by the retailer's mainframe, and electronically transmitted (EDI) to the vendor's computers. But in olden days, buyers signed PO's with pencils and pens. And if the buyer didn't like your merchandise, they didn't pick up their pencil to write you an order. So, although you may have the greatest product ever invented since the dinosaurs left the planet, unless you motivate the buyer to lift their pencil and "sign" or give you a PO, you don't complete your objective.

What power the buyer has in their hand—the power of the pencil! They have the power to order your goods and make you successful and rich, or they can pass you by, as if you don't exist, and give PO's to your competition. It's bad enough not to complete the sale, but to lose business to your competition is the final indignity, don't you think?

So, the buyer does have a tremendous amount of power. But I believe that salespeople have power too. Win the game. It's your choice.

Chapter 2

The Retail Sales Warrior

The traveling salesman who can sell the world the Brooklyn Bridge every day, can put anything over on you and convince you that tomatoes grow at the South Pole.

Ishmael Reed
author

Before we climb inside the buyer's skull for a quick exploration with flashlights, let me tell you something about them all. They come from the "show me" state, watching and waiting for the moves of salespeople. Many buyers believe that salespeople will try to sell them something that they don't terribly need. It's your job to get the buyer to have faith in your actions, for you to build credibility with them and to connect precisely with their requirements. If you don't establish trust in your relationship with them, you're just another fly by night salesperson.

So all buyers are cautiously viewing your style. The retail sales warrior establishes their worth every time they interact with the buyer. Get past the objections and show them that you're reliable, intelligent and seeking solutions to their problems. Oh yes, you also have the goods that their customers desire.

For you to be successful with buyers, you must intimately understand how they think. All of them—and this includes the tiny mom and pop buyers all the way up to the behemoth beast superstore buyers—use basically the same buying principles. Now, I know that someone reading this is chuckling because they've run into a buyer without any principles—lacking all of these skills. Sure, of course, those buyers are out there too, mucking up the works for every poor salesperson unfortunate enough to call on them.

In life, and in the ranks of buyers, yes, you are going to find good and bad ones, and folks who are totally inept as well. You will meet slick, highly skilled buyers and scum sucking, brain dead cretins. Retailing is a representation of society, so you do get the cross section of intelligent or abysmally stupid folks filling the buying ranks. Depending on the economy, it can be tough to get good people to join your company. I've worked in some of the most beautiful cities in America and, let me tell you, that doesn't help you to get better buyers.

Anyhow, buyers do come in all shapes and sizes and abilities, and each one, regardless of the company they work for, conducts themselves somewhat differently and has differing levels of organization. But they ALL utilize very similar buying principles. I'm going to reveal all those principles to you in this book.

You'd think that some retailing genius would have taken all these wonderful ways of doing business and carved it into stone for all to read. That would be too easy and retailers are all fighters and accustomed to walking a tough road. So you won't find any text that has all the retail detail. Instead, these principles are passed down verbally from the merchandise managers to the buyers, from the buyer to their assistants, and from the assistants down to the lowly trainees. The assistants and trainees are the ones kept locked in a padded room, with no light, and only vending machines and stress to keep them alive.

What am I going to do? I'm going to tell you these principles, these secrets, the way the buyer thinks. With this knowledge, you will walk the walk and talk the talk with buyers. If you totally understand the buyer and their principles, you will be able to communicate with them at a much higher level. You could sell more merchandise to them. They might actually be impressed with your approach. You could be tagged as a consummate professional. You might increase your standard of living. At the very least, you'll get pleasure watching the buyer's jaw drop when you talk to them about, "building an assortment designed to damage their competition, and fitting totally within their budget plan."

Before we have you spouting off brilliant platitudes, you need to answer the following question, critical to your success with retail buyers. Why does a buyer favor one salesperson more than others, especially when the buyer has a plethora of choices?

Do you know?

They pick the salesperson that takes them out to lunch. All right, that's a joke. Buyers do have reasons they prefer one vendor over another.

Qualities of the Best Salespeople

When I was a buyer, I had a standard that I used to measure the best salespeople. They had to have **quality** merchandise because I didn't want to infuriate customers and didn't want the goods to be returned to my store due to quality issues. Also, the merchandise had to arrive **on time** into my stores or warehouses—I didn't have time to chase shipments. Great **competitive pricing** was also critical. I also wanted a vendor who was on the **cutting edge**, ahead of other manufacturers, so that carrying their products in my store made my company cutting edge as well. Finally, I required salespeople

7

and manufacturers with good **communications skills**. Time was at a premium, and if the salesperson understood the mission of my store and my specific needs, and could communicate thoughts to his company and back to me, that was a thing of beauty. It made the buying job that much easier. Low-maintenance.

Buyers today don't have the time for teaching you what they want and need for their stores. They barely have time to do their jobs and don't enjoy hand holding untrained vendors. As a buyer, when I'd encounter a difficult to manage vendor or salesperson, it might take a year or two, but I would ultimately get even. Working with a vendor on a few points was fine, but if a salesperson required an inordinate amount of attention, that was torturing me and limiting my effectiveness, and killing my time.

What happened to folks who understood my language, the requirements we buyers had?

WADAYA THINK? I'd give them lots more business. I'd transfer business from the weaker vendor. Get the point? Keep it easy for the buyer and they just might like you and give you business. Make their life hell and they're likely to return the favor.

Things I will be teaching you in this book:

1. how to understand the buyer for fun and profit
2. how to kill your competition (but not literally)
3. how to become a retail samurai salesperson

I will be quoting from Miyamoto Musashi, an incredible Japanese samurai warrior, skilled swordsman, and a philosopher who had brilliant strategies for winning battles. Musashi was a samurai who lived to tell about it. His thinking dates back to 1650, but it is fresh and applicable to the competitive wars we fight in the retail business marketplace.

Also, no doubt you've noticed that I bolded a statement in the first chapter. **Think like a merchant or forever be a peddler.** Guess what? I have a bunch of significant thoughts sprinkled throughout this book. They are intended to make you think about how you conduct your business, how you compete in the marketplace and how you relate to the retail buyer.

Here's the second thought critical to the success of the retail sales warrior:

THOUGHT #2

Wrongly viewed among people of the world, not understanding anything is itself considered emptiness. This is not real emptiness; it is all delusion.[1]

Miyamoto Musashi

Mushashi's point is critical. Things you don't understand can appear to be unimportant, as if they don't exist, that only emptiness is there. However, these details can be critical and can hurt you. A samurai salesperson pays attention to all information around them, making certain that they understand what is taking place. Samurai's won't delude themselves.

If you want to be a samurai salesperson, successfully winning every battle, vanquishing your enemies, then I am here to help you. Do you want to sell more merchandise? Let's work better with these gatekeepers, the retail buyers.

Retail Samurai Salesperson

How would you define a retail samurai salesperson? Do you merely walk around in Japanese warrior garments? Do you adopt a sneering countenance, an air of superiority? Do you consider adding a sword to your wardrobe? NO! Clothing and an attitude won't make you a samurai. If you have time, read about the rich tradition of the samurai and how they upheld the highest virtues of their society. You shouldn't trivialize the samurai. If you become a samurai, no one will trivialize you either.

Here's my definition of a **RETAIL SAMURAI SALESPERSON.** For one, this sales professional is disciplined and operates almost in a stealth-like fashion. You are flying below the radar of your company, doing everything possible to be supportive of the buyer. I'm not talking about breaking the rules, but you are fighting to make things happen for the buyer, and you let the buyer know that. Don't settle for the typical bureaucratic bull that is commonplace today. Slice through that red tape with your figurative samurai sword.

The retail samurai salesperson is highly knowledgeable about the customer, the retailer, the marketplace and, of course, knows everything about the products they are selling. You have a warrior attitude and that should mean not tolerating mediocrity, slow movement within your company or any lack of support for you. Obviously, don't forget about corporate politics and swashbuckle your way out of a job. You need to be a samurai salesperson with tact.

9

Part of being supportive to the buyer includes proper follow through. That means *make it happen*. Remember the word "time." The buyer doesn't have the time to stay on top of you. Follow through and make their wishes and dreams come true. If you are a do-er rather than a talker, you will get along famously with the buyer. Make a commitment and follow it through until it is completed. Don't let any detail escape you. Just as the retail samurai buyers are fighting to the death for their companies, they expect you to do the same for them. Go down swinging and you'll earn their respect.

Retail Samurai Salespeople are ruthless with their competition too. Just don't splatter the buyer with any blood. Be sensitive to the type of buyer across the desk from you. Many buyers don't like to hear a salesperson bad-mouthing their competition. Know your customer before you say something irresponsible.

The best retail samurai salespeople have talent and they know how to drive their sales. It isn't a matter of luck. Yes, timing is critical, but they have everything in place for success. They are prepared for winning and ready when opportunity comes along.

Mushashi, the samurai, says if you want to follow his approach, you need to do the following:

THOUGHT #3

1. **Think of what is right and true.**
2. **Practice and cultivate the science.**
3. **Become acquainted with the arts.**
4. **Know the principles of the crafts.**
5. **Understand the harm and benefit in everything.**
6. **Learn to see everything accurately.**
7. **Become aware of what is not obvious.**
8. **Be careful even in small matters.**
9. **Do not do anything useless.**[2]

Miyamoto Musashi

The retail samurai salesperson has specific qualifications that make them perfect for the job. They follow an ethical path. Knowledge has been obtained that makes them an expert about the products they sell and about their company. They are keenly aware of what position their competition is taking in the marketplace, they are following all moving objects, and have strategies for dealing with them. Finally, they know everything about their customer—the buyer. The successful salesperson must understand the buyer and what items the buyer needs. Samurai salespeople sweat the small details and handle them before they get to the buyer's desk. They also are focused on specific objectives and do not let irrelevant projects interfere with their goals.

With so many breeds of salespeople lurking around a retailing buying office, how can you tell a superior salesperson from one that is more reptilian in nature? A sales pro, a retail samurai salesperson, is a very confident, self-motivated, self-starter. Usually they are happy, fun loving, intelligent and articulate. The best sales folks see the cup as half full.

Such a salesperson relishes their freedom, and enjoys operating independently in an assigned territory. They get a thrill by overcoming landmines thrown at them by their competition. Warrior salespeople offer quality products, provide market and competitive knowledge, outstanding service, and continuous follow up. The buyer's needs always are met and satisfied.

Furthermore, a successful salesperson must be a consultant to his customers, routinely solving problems for them. Faster than the swish of a samurai sword, the warrior-salesperson must eradicate anything that might compromise the sale of the merchandise, such as roadblocks in shipping, a shortage of goods, etc. If the salesperson's services can solve these problems, the retail buyer can stock their shelves and the end users can purchase the goods. It's beautiful to behold. Imagine that—selling goods and delivering them on time.

Of course, the samurai salesperson must have the merchandise that customers want to buy—goods that connote quality, have meaningful features and benefits, and must be fairly priced. Did you get that laundry list of requirements? Do you regularly provide all that to your customers?

Let's talk in greater detail about the requirements to long-term success, keeping your job and ensuring that the paychecks keep on coming. This includes ethics, company and product knowledge, understanding your competition and, crucially, who is the buyer and how should you interact with them?

Ethics

Ethics can be defined as principles, morals, values and beliefs. However, the word also is attached to taking the higher ground, rising above negativity and focusing on the greater good. If you operate on an ethical plane, you are far removed from corruption and the seamier side of business. Being an ethical salesperson is a good thing.

Ethics and integrity are critical to your continuing success as a businessperson. People easily recognize an unscrupulous salesperson and members of your industry will talk. Gossip-mongers will love spreading the

11

latest horror stories about you. Anything that gives off the appearance of being unethical should be avoided like the plague. When you move from one career position to another, all that you take with you are some skills, your integrity—and your reputation. Make certain that they remember you in a positive light.

Unethical shortcuts may work in the short term, but are long-term land mines and they will come back to explode when you can least afford it. Keep your nose clean (and the rest of your body as well). A dishonest person is untrustworthy regardless of all other positive character traits. Haven't you known people that you liked, but you wouldn't trust them with your life? Why was that? Had they ever done something slightly underhanded to you or someone you knew? Could they ever escape that brand?

You don't want to be connected to these people.

Product and Company Knowledge

What about the power that comes from expert knowledge of your products and your company? You may get tired hearing that knowledge is power, but have you known powerful people who didn't possess some knowledge? Knowledge is an extremely powerful asset for the samurai salesperson. If you examine the battlefield strategies of Miyamoto Musashi, you notice that he is constantly evaluating his surroundings, drawing conclusions from what he is experiencing. The more knowledge Mushashi had about his environment, the more powerful he became as a warrior. What's most impressive is that Musashi fought numerous battles and lived to write about it. Emulate a winner, learn from your experiences, and be an expert on your products. One retail merchant from my past would say, "be a student of your business."

Help the buyer; be there with guidance and support. Offer superior company and product knowledge. If you totally have studied your competition as well, you will be able to outperform them. Think about how your products and services can benefit your customer. Make sure that you communicate those positive attributes to the buyer. Let them know how committed you are to helping them to drive their sales.

Know Your Competition

You are propelling the business and are constantly looking over your shoulder, watching the moves of your competition. They'd like nothing better than to watch you back up over some deeply hidden mine. Ker-POW!!! Watch out for your competition. YOU ARE AT WAR WITH

YOUR COMPETITION. Although there are kinder and gentler times in business, and you do see competitors working together, is there a compelling reason to believe that your competition wants to help you? Or would they prefer seeing you skewered and spinning on a spit over an open fire. Trust me, your competitors won't be singing songs with you around the campfire. Watch your back with your competition, and keep your customer aware of their activities too. After all, you are a superior, finely honed sales machine.

Be sure to research your primary competitors and become intimate with their products. Look at this merchandise from a customer/buyer's perspective. Does the competition have a better product or a superior feature? What makes the competition's products desirable? Be sure to measure their product's quality against your offerings—quality to quality.

One of my favorite meetings with an "informed" salesperson was when they measured their goods against the competition. "Ours is superior because...," invariably started the statement. Then they'd try to show me how an inferior product from their competition didn't measure up to the wonderful merchandise they'd deposited on my desk. However, their full-featured item for $100 was competing with a product missing features but retailing for $50. Yet the $50 one was likely to outsell its more expensive relative.

Superiority doesn't equal more sales. How will the consumer judge the merchandise? If you are selling with blinders on, and ignoring your competition, the marketplace and the buyer's intelligence, then you might as well give up sales for a career. The most successful mass-market stores today sell "good" merchandise and people love shopping for them. Not every consumer wants the top quality. Think like a consumer.

While examining your competition, be sure to research their products and point of view until you find a specific advantage over them—then decide how to exploit that. Let's suppose that you're selling dog food at a premium price. You better have a really fine story delineating all the superlatives about your products vs. brand X. For example, does your food possess all natural ingredients and maintain the dog's bone structure? Have a detailed analysis of your product as compared to your competition. But how will all natural ingredients benefit the dog? Although it seems obvious, make sure that you clearly explain it to the buyer, because the buyer will need to explain it to his store sales personnel. If you're charging a higher price than the competition, what is the justification? Do you have a superior product and will the consumer comprehend that? Or will Joe Consumer think that you produce ridiculously expensive goods?

Become a detective and learn everything you can about what competitors are doing. Be certain that you follow-up and insure that your service is superior to other manufacturers in that category. If you are always filling orders on time with great selling items, it is likely that you will stand out from your competition.

Who is the Buyer?

Let's examine another significant point. Who is the buyer? How much do you really know about them? To do this properly, you need to turn into a detective. Now, in this information age, I don't mean going online and pulling up a credit report on them. I also wouldn't follow them around their neighborhood on weekends. But you can find out all kinds of information by asking them and their associates—what does the buyer like? What is their background?

Speak with people in the industry about the buyer. Does the buyer like sports or gourmet food or a special kind of music? Salespeople who used to suck up to me would take me out for very high-end meals. All they had to do was ask me what I enjoyed doing. But it is possible to mishandle this information. One salesman heard that I loved listening to music. One day, I returned to my office and found an opera CD sitting in the middle of my desk, with a card from this vendor. He had committed several mistakes with this transaction: one, it was against my company policy to accept gifts; two, he never asked what kind of music I listened to, which showed that he really wasn't much of a detective; and three, I absolutely abhor opera. So, you can give the salesperson credit for trying, but not trying that terribly hard.

For all the better salespeople/detectives out there, what does the buyer's office tell you? Do they have family pictures, are awards posted, do they belong to clubs, and are special sayings quoted on the walls? What can you learn about the gatekeeper when you're in their inner sanctum? Take an instant impression of the surroundings and decide what "vibe" you get from their office. Utilize this information to your advantage.

Realize that your first meeting with the buyer has to accomplish your objectives—completing a sale. You probably won't have a second chance, so first impressions count. Speak with authority and make sure that you did all your homework. And for the sake of every buyer in America, be meticulous with your personal hygiene and appearance. I've lost count of the number of bad smelling salespeople I've encountered. It usually is bad breath, but body odor occasionally plays a part. Don't let your wardrobe from 1990 and your tie or dress with a pizza stain derail a great performance with the buyer. If you're uncertain how to dress, either send me a Polaroid for evaluation, or ask your significant other for some assistance. Buyers may not be devout followers of haute couture, but they can detect someone dressing like a circus clown from 50 feet away. If you dress like a jerk, you might not have proper business-sense either. It's your call if you'd care to risk being typed that way.

Whether it's your first meeting with a buyer or the 99th, every session counts. Enter the meeting room with a smile, maintain eye contact and project a friendly demeanor. Be sure to exude confidence. Take an instant impression of your surroundings. Is the buyer listening to you? What is the body language telling you? Non-verbal communication will tell you a great deal. Is the buyer unconscious and snoring up a storm? The far away look in their eye doesn't mean that they are falling in love with you. Be a samurai and pay attention to the atmosphere. Are the arms and legs crossed? That is not good body language—the buyer is putting up a barrier to your presentation.

So how can you get the buyer to join you in the "comfort zone?" How can you get them to let down their guard? Depending on the buyer's personality, there are a variety of approaches. Can you utilize humor to break the ice? Get the buyer laughing if it's possible. What kind of emotion do you feel in their office? Do you feel negativity? Or are they just being resistant to your presentation? Remember, buyers see innumerable presentations in their lifetime from salespeople who promise things impossible to deliver. Buyers today are jaded—they've heard it all and seen it all. You've got to be sure that you can substantiate all your claims. The gatekeeper would like to be "wowed," but they've attended many substandard presentations that failed to deliver. If you can impress them with the product, your knowledge or your interesting approach, you will get to the comfort zone that much faster.

What if you sense negativity? What is the cause of it? You need to establish if the buyer is too busy and, if so, cut directly to the chase. If that's not the case, you have my full permission to schmooze. Let me define that term for folks that haven't experienced schmoozing. You may talk their ear off, if they are responsive to it. You may wax eloquent, if the buyer is receptive. Hell, you can deliver the Gettysburg Address if it will get your line proper attention from the buyer.

There are subjects that any intelligent salesperson will avoid: politics and religion. You never know the innermost thoughts of a buyer, and they probably will never share them with you. Why should they? Are they your best friend? So, if you let it slip that you think the republicans are wonderful, without fail the buyer will be a democrat. If you have devout religious beliefs, invariably the buyer will have a different point of view.

You also need to be careful with your more colorful expressions and curse words. I've seen a great meeting lose its luster when a salesman decided to insert a four-letter word into the conversation. The buyer he was

15

addressing was supremely offended, but never told him. Instead, she gave the cold shoulder to his business.

Let's return to the main reason you meet with the buyer—to close a sale. Now, this sale could require multiple visits, or might even take a long time to finalize. If the buyer is happy with the existing vendor, you might try swimming upstream instead. But you need to assume that you can close the sale potentially that day. You're closing from the moment you enter the meeting room. Begin your presentation, check for vital signs emanating from the buyer (like a pulse), and head for the close.

Negotiation

Closing sales will involve some level of negotiation with the buyer, and most buyers relish the opportunity to wrangle a deal out of you. All buyers are paid to negotiate the best deal possible for their store. Depending on the buyer's personality and skill level, the bargaining process could be matter of fact, laid back, or they could haggle back and forth until they've drained you of money and blood.

Buyers are responsible for negotiating prices, financial incentives, rebate, advertising monies (coop), and any extra funds available. You must always make them feel like they are improving their financial position with you.

There are numerous methods for negotiating deals and you'll experience them all when you go to visit the buyer. Realize, however, that most buyers would like to consummate some arrangement with you; they don't get any credit for sitting on their hands.

If you understand that the word "negotiation" is married to the buyer, you will have mastered part of the battle. Buyers love to negotiate. So, let them feel like they're winning. Maybe you can't give them all ten things they've requested, but certainly you need to give them one or two. Buyers who leave a negotiation and have nothing to show for the effort are not held in high esteem by their management. Every meeting with them should move the plan forward, sprinkling in a win, here and there.

A negotiation can finish in one meeting or take years to complete—it depends on the buyer, their workload and the level of complexity of the deal. Try to close the transaction quickly, but be ready for the long haul.

One common trait among buyers is that they all have egos and you do need to stroke them. This is "selling 101," and you should understand how to listen to them talk, respond to their needs and make them feel important.

Be prepared for the more difficult negotiations. You'll experience sessions that take lots of time to finalize. Also, you'll run into some very difficult types of buyers. Wearing down a vendor is part of the tricks that buyers employ to get what they want. Utilizing "stall" tactics or bringing irrelevant issues into the session can derail a salesperson's focus and potentially give the buyer a win. For example, if a buyer wants a better price and you're unwilling to give it to them, the buyer could complain about your service or the special treatment you are giving to their competition. If they can make you feel guilty, you'll bend to their demands. It's one of many tricks they can employ.

You will encounter many different buyer personalities, and we will discuss them in detail in the next chapter. Your job is to adjust your approach based on the personality and skill of the buyer, and make them all feel like winners.

Chapter 3
Deep Inside the Retail Buyer's Cranium

THOUGHT #4

It is important to start by setting these broad principles in your heart, and train in the Way of strategy. If you do not look at things on a large scale it will be difficult for you to master strategy. If you learn and attain this strategy you will never lose even to twenty or thirty enemies. More than anything to start with you must set your heart on strategy and earnestly stick to the Way.

You will come to be able to actually beat men in fights, and to be able to win with your eye. Also by training you will be able to freely control your own body, conquer men with your body, and with sufficient training you will be able to beat ten men with your spirit. When you have reached this point, will it not mean that you are invincible? [3]

Miyamoto Musashi

The invincible gatekeeper who guards the purchasing for corporations is the enemy to some salespeople, while some folks are able to master and control this relationship. Let's get deep inside the buyer's brain, learn to understand their motivations and how to work better with them. If the buyer/seller relationship is adversarial, you can forget driving your sales to a higher level. We need to examine the various types of buyer's personalities you are likely to encounter and detail the conditions you'll find in most buying offices.

It's time to take a step deep inside the buyer's cranium, a frightening place to be for some salespeople. Are buyers rational businesspeople? Some of them are. Are some disorganized? Certainly. Well, what kind of personalities will you experience?

Can you describe all the different types of buyers and buying styles that you have encountered? It is infinitely more complicated than "good buyers" and "bad buyers." I've been in the buying trenches and seen all types at many companies. In fact, some of the personalities I describe below fit me perfectly.

So what are the different types of buyers? I detail eight styles of buying, but you're likely to come across mixtures or hybrids as well.

Eight Types of Buyers

The first buyer I'd like to introduce to you is my favorite, the new buyer to a category, **SLASH and BURN**. Often, this type of buyer has been in retailing for a few years, and has handled other departments. But they have been infected with "new buyer-itis." Old relationships are cast to the wind without regard to the impact. You say you've been selling a retailer for 10 years or more and now the new buyer doesn't seem to like you? It's an old story. Many buyers approach existing vendors with reverence, but the slash and burn buyer could care less about all the accommodations this vendor has given. That's past tense to this person. Some other buyer with limited skills must have selected the current vendor. This type of buyer has no regard for your business and, like a dog marking his territory, wants to establish *their* vendor structure. If they didn't create the vendor mix, then they can't be comfortable with it.

Clearly, this kind of buying approach can damage a store's reputation and merchandise content. But many times this is happening below the radar, and no one at the retailer is aware of the occurrence. You are put into a quandary here. Do you relax and hope that this situation will improve? But what if it doesn't? Do you go over the buyer's head and speak with their boss?

At times like these, you certainly have to weigh all the consequences. If you do nothing, is it likely to continue? Are you willing to watch as this buyer slices off a piece of your business and hands it to someone else? If not, you should attempt to reason with the buyer and try to understand why this is occurring. Perhaps you have done something to injure the relationship, like a poor on-time shipping record. Is there a way that you can show the new buyer how you can change a few things to make it more to their liking? Try adapting to the new buyer if you can. If this isn't the case, do you know the buyer's merchandise manager and can you have an "off the record" talk? Here's the best advice: if doing nothing will cause you pain and loss of business, what do you have to lose by talking with the buyer's boss? Is there a likelihood that the buyer will get infuriated? Yes, but what choice do you have? You can hope that the merchandise manager is skillful enough to present the events in a non-threatening way to his buyer. Try to prevent further destruction before it goes too far.

Then, there's buyer type #2—**THE NICE GUY/GAL.** This kind of buyer loves going out to lunch with you, but never gives you bad news. They won't pull the trigger and are totally non-committal. But they enjoy meeting with you and are a pleasure to have a conversation with. Yet you'll never accomplish anything with them. Now, if you contrast this style to the slash and burn buyer, obviously buildings aren't exploding around you—it's

19

not a catastrophic relationship. However, this buyer won't help you to be a hero either; you're not going to achieve champion sales results while this buyer is in control.

I remember working for a very large national retail chain, and one of my vendors took me aside one day, asking for advice. Another buyer in my company was stonewalling this vendor, and never added any merchandise. This buyer would tell his suppliers that a product or concept was nice and that he'd like "to think about it." Whether a buyer is "sleeping on it" or "thinking about it," the end result is the same—nothing is happening. While walking the floor of a tradeshow months later, the CEO of my company was accosted by 5 vendors who ranted about this buyer's ineptitude, requesting the CEO's help. The CEO was mortified. A few days after this buyer was fired, we discovered over 100 forms in his desk for adding new items to the assortment, but he never followed through and ordered the merchandise.

You probably could do a psychological analysis of this buying style and conclude that they fear change, love the status quo, don't want to have conflict, hate to deliver bad news or don't know how to move projects forward. You don't need Sigmund Freud to tell you that this buyer is not helping you to achieve your next sales bonus check. Unfortunately, most retailers have some buyer stuck in this rut and they need to help them to change their evil ways. But, like the slash and burn buyer, this nice guy/gal may not be ruffling any feathers internally, so they can operate this way, unchallenged, for a while.

Try setting a deadline with this buyer and call them on it. Be aggressive and don't let them slip through your hands. Are they willing to test your product or concept initially in a few stores? See if you can get them to give you a concrete reason for their reticence. If this still doesn't move the project forward, can you talk with their boss? Lack of change is death to retailers. No customer wants to enter a retail store that has the same boring stuff on the shelf all the time. Change and new items keep a store fresh and vibrant. I'm sure that most merchandise managers would be receptive to your plight. Chances are that they'd be very unhappy to learn that their buyer isn't taking any risks in order to improve the business.

Moving on to buyer personality #3, we introduce to you **THE ANALYST**.

More and more retailers are filling their buying ranks with this kind of individual. "Can you quantify that?" asks the analyst-buyer. Clearly, business today requires people to study the sales of their products and respond accordingly. Yet, how many of you have been in the analysis/paralysis zone?

This buyer lives only in a world of numbers. Products don't have any features and benefits; all the analyst-buyer is interested in is how many pieces can be sold. Forget about your merchandise rounding out an assortment of existing items on the shelves. Forget about it being fashionable. Forget about being the first to carry it. None of those sales pitches will work. Everything must be proven financially. One solution is to schedule a test with this product, or to detail how many pieces the competition is selling. If this should fail, be sure to show the merchandise to the buyer's upper management when they walk past your booth at a tradeshow. Yes, you did offer these goods to their buyer a long time ago.

Buyer #4 is appropriately called **THE KID**. The wonderful thing about retailing is that very young people are hired into managing million dollar businesses and allowed to make decisions. That can be quite a rush and ego trip if you're 26 years old. However, unless buying skills are imparted within the womb, this type of individual is "green," or "wet behind the ears." A more politically correct word would be "inexperienced."

You do find some exceptional young buyers out there and I've had the pleasure to associate with these retailing wunderkinds. There are folks who are naturally adept at the buying process. Trace the career paths of merchandising wizards like Allen Questrom, currently the CEO for JC Penney, who turned around Federated Department Stores and bought his competitor, Macys. He started as a trainee for the now-deceased Abraham & Straus, New York. I was fortunate to have been part of Richs, Atlanta, when he was CEO there. He'd take a group of his buyers up to the executive chambers and talk about merchandise and why it made sense for our store to sell it. You could see the sparkle in his eyes when he discussed products. Mr. Questrom didn't download information to us; rather, he'd ask us questions to get us thinking. It always was an eye opening experience. Allen Questrom was destined to be a retailing legend.

It can be exasperating if you're stuck selling anyone who isn't as talented as Mr. Questrom. Many retailers today don't train their teams, preferring on the job experiences to hone their abilities. This is a hit or miss approach to growing business skills, but there's no point in complaining about it. When you're faced with the inexperience of a kid buyer, what can you do? For one, be patient and try to guide them along. The positive point of view here is that you can mold them to your thinking. The other side is that a green buyer could also display characteristics of the nice guy/gal and be totally ineffectual. This buyer also requires heavier hand-holding. Usually, salespeople with positive attitudes are able to forge a winning relationship with kid buyers. Respect these buyers, empower them, teach them and be careful. Most kid buyers will remember your assistance and kindness and try to return the favor.

Lurking behind all the other buyers, you can spot a rare species, buyer #5, **SHY and CEREBRAL**. I've known a few buyers like this. One gal I met in my department store days probably would have preferred being a research assistant or librarian. There was nothing dynamic about her–but she was extremely nice. In the buying jungle—where it's eat or be eaten—it is rare to find buyers like this, but they do exist. They may not hold illuminating conversations with you, they are probably afraid to challenge you, and I'm convinced that some of them are scared of the sound of their own voice. Approach them with care and be respectful of their space. Try to draw them gently out of their cocoon. I have seen many successful interactions with this unique type of buyer. They take a little longer to get to know because of their timidity. Persistence on your part will yield rewards and help them to reach a comfort zone with you. However, you won't find too many shy and cerebral buyers out there. The retail environment is not suited for this buyer type.

How do you approach buyer #6, **THE SEASONED PRO**? This buyer is a war-hardened veteran, having survived intact despite traveling from position to position for a multitude of retailers. For a long time, I thought that my experiences were unique; that it was unusual to have worked for more than 6 retailers, and to have lived in 5 US states. But this is normal in today's business climate. Companies come and go, management changes and either lays waste to their talent structure, or motivates these employees to move on. Retail Samurai Merchants have earned their stripes. I've known buyers, who were 50 years old or more and have traversed the United States during their careers. Some buyers grow old gracefully with a single company, although this is rare. One seasoned professional that I met worked for over 20 years as a book buyer for a department store chain. She was worldly wise and eccentric, but she knew every facet of the book business. You couldn't scam her, nor would you ever dare—she'd put you in your place. But if you had merchandise with great value, were sincere in your presentation, consistently reliable, and spoke to her with respect and intelligence, she responded warmly to that approach.

Theoretically, it should be the easiest to interact with the seasoned pro buyer. After all, you don't have to train this person; you can communicate at a higher level and they've gotten to this position because they have an efficient style in their dealings with salespeople. Normally, this is all true, but on occasion there are deviations. For example, you can find a well-seasoned buyer that is afflicted with nice guy/gal syndrome, or they can be overly analytical, intimidating, or have a no nonsense approach. On the positive side, many of these buyers have left their egos at the door, having endured innumerable battles, and are very comfortable with their styles and don't need to prove their qualifications to you.

For the samurai sales professional, the seasoned pro buyer should be a pleasure. However, you must understand the level of detail required before setting foot into their office. If you don't truly comprehend how to interact with this type of buyer, you need to do one of three things: one, don't walk into their office until you are ready; two, speak with other salespeople who have successfully called on this buyer; or, three, if all else fails and you're desperate, call and hire me to teach you how to be prepared. Meeting with a seasoned buyer can be a stroll through a nature preserve, or it can be a journey of terror, lost deep in the jungle without a map, without food or a compass. Be fully equipped to meet with the seasoned pro, be respectful and never be condescending. You could be rewarded with a wonderful relationship and a nice chunk of business.

Do you enjoy jamming power tools into your body? Steel yourself to the crushing power of buyer # 7, **THE BULLDOZER**. What did you say? You hear the sound of trees crashing, bones breaking and people screaming? Why, of course you do—there's a bulldozer on the loose, and it's wreaking havoc everywhere it goes. This type of buyer will run over you, won't listen, and keeps charging. The word "pushy" doesn't begin to cover their domineering style—they are impelled to get their own way and love to force you to do as they command. The bulldozer buyer is in a perfect spot to utilize their skills; salespeople have to delicately follow the leader or potentially jeopardize their business. This buyer is usually immature and thriving on power, almost like "the kid" buyer with a really bad attitude and an ego out of control.

How can you deal with such a miserable person? The samurai salesperson needs to employ their wisdom, patience and subjugate their ego in the presence of the bulldozer. You can't have two strong-willed people going at it here, or you're asking for a steel cage match and some blood will spill. This won't be good for your business. Humor this kind of buyer, but don't patronize them. Ask for their advice, make suggestions that they can amplify and make their own. Let them be the important, all knowing, retailing genius. If they have half a brain, they'll either improve eventually, or slide down the slippery slope, eventually getting caught by the store's management. In short, work with them carefully, but keep your distance.

When the bulldozer doesn't mature, but is able to continue on their wretched path, they might evolve to a lower life form, aptly named **THE INTIMIDATOR**, buyer # 8. Here, you will be threatened with the loss of your job, loss of business and loss of your life, unless things are exactly the way they want it. This buyer has a mean streak a mile wide and often does have a high degree of intelligence, making them more dangerous. But this person must have suffered some irreparable damage to their psyche somewhere along the way, and now they're taking their misery out on you. There are other wonderful traits that these folks have, including seething emotions, screaming, and the ability to ridicule. They are just a joy to be around.

At the beginning of chapter one, I offered a tale for your amusement about a meeting between a nasty intimidating buyer (me) and the vice president of sales who nearly encountered cardiac arrest. That buyer wasn't satisfied with solely communicating dissatisfaction—no, he had to impact the salesman's ego too. Unfortunately, today's buyers are under so much pressure, with crushing workloads, that it does affect the way they treat people. They're a little persnickety. Corporations love to keep their general and administrative expenses low which, in turn, places an unfair burden on the worker bees. At one organization, the responsibility previously shared by three people was funneled down to two sadly overwrought individuals. I was one of the two stressed people. Sadly, I wasn't always charming to be around. I'd like to believe that intimidator buyers aren't bad through and through, just highly stressed out.

Working for one department store, I inherited a boss who enjoyed intimidating his buyers and any supplier without a thick skin. He would scream at people until his face turned red. If you caught a glimpse of his expression when he'd leave the area of devastation, you'd find him smirking. Many intimidating buyers get pleasure out of torturing other human beings. The question you need to ask yourself is: "Can this buyer follow through on the threats?" If you are able to toss off their comments as immaturity or a warped way of operating, you'll be healthier for it and your business won't be impacted.

You have several choices here. One, you can try to work with this lunatic and let their diatribe roll off your back. Two, you can fling their crap back at them and see what happens. With some intimidators, this is what they expect—they try to see how far they can push you. But scooping the mud and hurling it back takes a lot of courage. Unless you have a good reason to believe that this will produce positive results, be careful with this strategy. Three, you can cautiously approach their boss, dropping hints that you are getting abused. Four, if the treatment is that outrageous, I'd recommend getting your boss on the telephone with the buyer's supervisor. I do not believe that anyone was put on this planet to be someone else's whipping post. If you feel that you are being mistreated, fight back. Yes, they are the customer and the customer is always right, but whether it is sexual abuse or verbal abuse, it is still uncalled for in the workplace.

Positive Confrontation

What is the quality of your relationship with the buyer? Do you have issues that are impacting your business? Are you comfortable with your buyer so you can discuss these problems? Or has the buyer sufficiently frightened the crap out of you and every meeting with them is filled with dread? Obviously, if you are interacting with a slash and burn buyer, or a bulldozer, or an intimidator, you have a difficult road to hoe. Every step must feel like you're walking on eggshells. But you are a samurai salesperson and fear should not be part of your thoughts. If you have a truly tough business situation, are you secure enough with your approach and the relationship you have with the buyer to broach any subject?

I believe in "positive confrontation." Yes, I know that confrontation has negative connotations for most of you. A war is a confrontation between opposing forces utilizing weapons designed to kill. Bringing people together to discuss issues is a confrontation, but it doesn't have to become a negative incident. I'm convinced that lots of folks don't like to have a heavy or difficult interaction, especially if emotions are involved or one side believes that someone is not treating them in a fair way. Dealing with an issue, face to face, mano a mano, is a tense event for some salespeople. But if everything was sweetness and light, and everything functioned smoothly, the world wouldn't need salespeople, right?

You need to be able to have positive confrontations with your buyers. This is free flowing dialog designed to improve a business relationship. It should be part of a relationship filled with reciprocity; you do some nice things for the buyer and they return the favor. You're having an issue with the promotion of your products—positive confrontation. You are getting tremendous pressure from your vice president of sales to get your new products into a retailer, but the buyer is moving very slowly—positive confrontation. The retail stores aren't putting your goods out on the selling floor—positive confrontation.

I would be delusional if I believed that every buyer in America would be receptive to positive confrontation. I realize that that isn't the case. But if something is *significantly* wrong at a particular retailer, you must deal with the problem. That is part of your responsibility. If you can't reason with the buyer, do you have a relationship with the buyer's boss, the merchandise manager? A samurai salesperson makes contact with many people within a retail organization, because that is a good business practice and you never know when you'll need additional support. Samurai warriors were not looking for confrontations, but they would deal with a conflict if they had to oppose a warring faction. Similarly, you should utilize positive confrontation to move your business forward with the buyer.

Negotiation

Expect to spend some time with the buyer in a give and take situation. You give and they take. Of course, that's a joke, but some buyers do operate in that fashion. Negotiation to them is grabbing all you can get from the vendor. Most buyers, however, understand that both parties must be satisfied for a negotiation to be considered a "win."

Realize that the buyer is on a hunt. If you give them a "trophy" to carry back to their management, a sign that they are superior negotiators, they will be proud and probably will enjoy doing business with you. If you are a difficult person to bargain with, and put up a never-ending struggle, you do run the risk of alienating the buyer.

All buyers love to win. Can you aid them in that pursuit?

Chapter 4

The Maelstrom is Called the Buying Office

Unless you have an appreciation for the buyer's working conditions, it is unlikely that you will be totally successful. When they don't complete your project on time or call you back, it's not only because they're busy. Other factors are impacting their time. Part of a good relationship with the buying team requires you to understand their daily schedule and environment.

For those of you who come to visit, the buying office probably seems like an intense place. People are scurrying around, popping heads into offices, there are multiple interruptions, and lots of noise and excitement. That's the face the corporations want you to see. However, some retailers won't let you into their buying offices, but instead will have you speak with the buyers in meeting rooms. A session with a vendor will discuss movement of product: "Will it sell?" or "Why isn't it selling?" or "How can I sell more?"

The buying office has many working parts, people and ideas in motion, projects in various states of completion or disarray. In the bowels of retail corporate headquarters, numerous meetings are taking place with internal personnel covering a multitude of topics: advertising design, budget planning, dealing with customer complaints and store operational issues, analyzing sales, building store layouts (planograms) and much more.

So, the buying office is a fun, exhilarating experience, right? Try asking a buyer that question. Many will tell you that, yes, they do have fun and moments of exultation. Dig a little further beneath the surface, get the buyer's friendship, and perhaps they'll tell you what the full body/mind experience is really like.

I've been a member of numerous buying offices, and there were similarities between them all. Some of the organizations had better business conditions or were more profitable. A few had superlative leadership, and all tried to attract outstanding talent in their buying ranks.

So, you ask, "Mr. Expert Merchant, what is the buying office really like?" The buying office is a tough place to work. Most of my experiences were great, but the buying office is a beast. It challenges you and pushes you, and that's good. But the buying office and their leadership show no mercy for the associates. One ex-department store buyer, who became famous leading a hard goods chain down in Florida, would say that buyers and their assistants should be thrown into a darkened, locked room and have raw meat thrown through the bars to keep them nourished. What is the buying office really like? It's like living hell for some people.

Drains on Buyer's Time

There is a long list of drains on the buyer's time. Let's cover a few of them. They're invited to long meetings examining corporate policy, advertising and budget planning, and many sessions have little application to them. Buyers must be really popular, because everyone in the corporate retail headquarters likes inviting them to their meetings. In several corporations that employed me, I added up all the hours for meetings that buyers were invited to, and how many hours of work the buyers had on their desks in an average week, and you know what? Some buyers required an 80-90 hour week to get their jobs done, and the meetings often took 25% of their time or more.

So, how do buyers prioritize their time? Some of them can't and are caught in the whirlwind experience spinning around them. A maelstrom is a violent whirlpool that ships at sea can encounter. The buying office can be like that at times—responsibilities swirling around the buyer's heads and sucking the unprepared into its vortex. Some buyers understand time management, carry electronic organizers and carefully allocate their time. The best buyers constantly re-evaluate their time, juggling their priority lists. Is it an "A" priority? Suddenly, projects that were categorized previously as "B" or "C" level are thrust to the top of the list due to management involvement or some other outside interference. They become "A" priorities. Buyers have to deal with this on a daily basis, and it can impact your project positively or negatively.

Your endeavor could be on the top of the heap and, out of the blue, another assignment leap frogs yours and hits the number one spot. Sometimes, nice projects don't make it to the top of the "to do" list—ever. I've had many salespeople complain to me that buyers don't get to their projects on a timely basis. I ask the salesperson to rate the importance of the task with all the other things on the buyer's plate. Then, I encourage the salesperson to rank how critical this issue is to their factory. If a slow moving project deserves a low importance rating, then I tell the salesperson to cool their jets. Ranting and raving to the buyer or buyer's boss about an incomplete low priority project is a sure sign that you don't have a clue about the buyer's workload. It also shows your total lack of sensitivity. Great relationships are not cultivated this way. On the other hand, if you really need the buyer's support on a project that has languished untouched for months, approach the buyer and explain your circumstances. Ask them if there's anything that you can do to help speed up the mission.

There are other elements that impact a buyer's time. Meetings today can last from four to eight hours. Have you recently been in an all day meeting?

28

How does your brain feel afterwards? I'm convinced that if you did a brain scan on a buyer after a long meeting, that brain would resemble a bowl of oatmeal, or maybe a slushee from a convenience store. Buyers constantly deal with long meetings and it is mind numbing. Try losing one half or one full day in a meeting and see how that would affect your productivity and your enthusiasm.

As if that weren't enough, buyers receive up to 100 emails per day and plenty of phone calls from their stores, vendors and coworkers within the corporate office. One overloaded buyer pointed out to me, "you can't just delete 100 emails. You have to open them and at least scan the contents quickly to see if you eliminate it." Even scanning emails quickly takes time out of their day. Add to this a constant stream of U.S. mail with offers from suppliers wanting to do business, and all kinds of boxes with samples for evaluation. Unopened sample boxes provide the decor for the hallways of most buying offices in America.

The Team and the Turnover

The people surrounding buyers also demand time. Buyers are managers and typically have a staff reporting to them. They're working with people under them: under-trained, under-paid and under-skilled. Many buyers in America are fortunate to have an assistant who knows the ropes and doesn't require much instruction. Ask your buyer about their team sometime.

Retail buying and merchandising is a high-powered and high-pressure existence and, as a result, has high turnover. Some retail chains have turnover "unofficially" built into their plans. By turning over the staff every few years, the buyer's point of view keeps shifting, keeping the merchandise fresh and forever changing, and that keeps their store exciting to the consumer. At least that's what some retail executives believe off the record. With constant turnover, it's more likely that your buyer has to regularly train an assistant, taking another bite out of the buyer's time. If the buyer is busy training their staff, then they're spending a whole lot less time adding your new items to the assortment.

Let's talk about the turnover of the buying team. This impacts the buyer's time and your productivity. I was chatting with a manufacturer the other day who was exasperated with the buyers from a major corporation. "As if it wasn't hard enough getting this store to buy my merchandise in the first place, and difficult to get to know all the buyers and merchandise management's likes and dislikes, then you get slammed with turnover of people." Yes, it's a hard road to hoe. You must get to know your buyers and get them to like you before they may buy your products. But you also will run into the chaos created by their departure.

How can you deal with the loss of your buyer? Make sure that you know the other buyers, merchandise managers, general merchandise manager, the vice president or senior vice president of merchandising. Do you have a relationship with the assistant buyer? Although an abrupt exit of a buyer can force many assistant buyers to sink under the workload, many assistants thrive under these circumstances and prove how valuable they are to the company. Talk with the assistant when the buyer bolts and ask for their support. Retailers do have succession plans—at least many of them do. Find out when a new buyer will be installed and if they are considering the assistant for a promotion into that spot.

If you don't have a relationship with the folks mentioned above, you won't be informed about the replacement buyer. What if you have a major project that had been started by the buyer before they flew the coop? Do you start calling people you don't know—like the buyer's boss—to introduce yourself and inquire about the progress of the task? Now, I know that some of you are shaking your heads, because all of this should be the obvious way to deal with turnover. But you'd be surprised how many folks don't have a proper relationship with the divisional merchandise manager or vice president of merchandising, or the assistant buyer. Even if you're a small player, you must get acquainted.

Unless your buyer is associated with a top retailer in America, many buyers are accustomed to sales information systems that don't always run smoothly, thus making it difficult to get data that's accurate or timely. The best retailers are known for state of the art computer systems with detailed information. Unfortunately, for the rest of America, many retailers have a way to go before their information is world class. This impacts the buyer's time. If you constantly have to dig to get information, how can you accurately and easily run your business? The more time a buyer needs to spend finding out how their products are performing, the less time they have to do other aspects of their jobs. Some buyers would quickly point out to me that, even if they had quality information that was easy to obtain, they still wouldn't have the time to analyze it anyway.

So when is the buyer able to do their jobs? When do they find the time to evaluate merchandise and sales data and meet with vendors to review new product opportunities? Interesting enough, at some retailers, management has to battle a buyer backlash—the buyers don't have time to meet with suppliers or time to prepare for vendor meetings. If they do have a get-together, some buyers are pressed to find the time to execute plans proposed during these vendor sessions.

Red Tape, Pressure and Politics

Part of the problem is the headquarters staff. There are folks who don't share the buyer's vision. It exasperates the buyer and the vendor, but today you need to motivate many internal persons to help get a project completed. Let's suppose the buyer purchased new merchandise from you. How are you going to sign the product in the stores? This requires the support of the sign department, store operations and others. If one member of the group doesn't feel like the task is important enough, they merely ignore it and hope it goes away. What if you've delivered great products in outstanding packaging and the buyer runs into a roadblock in the advertising department? Suppose that the team there presents the merchandise in an incomprehensible way in an ad? So buyers have to nag, cajole, and encourage teammates to support them. Buyers who are talented in pulling teams of people together, cutting through red tape and having clear direction, are the ones who succeed in this environment.

All this pressure has to manifest itself somewhere. Someday, someone will do a survey of retail buyers and find out if their jobs impact them at home. I'm sure that buyers aren't alone in this regard—anyone with a high-pressure position is subject to strained personal relationships too. How do some buyers deal with this stress? Buyers eat their young, those poor assistant buyers. Retail corporate management, in turn, eats the buyers. But the joy doesn't stop there. Some buyers will take their nervous tension out on you, some will internalize it, some roll with it, and some implode. KABOOM!!! Oops, just lost another buyer.

Fires are burning everywhere and every project is expected to be finished yesterday.

Other internal departments—advertising, operations and others—are making demands. Interruptions are constant.

Add politics on top of all those issues. Often it's not what you do; it's how you do it. If someone completes a project, but infuriates co-workers, it's not considered a good job. At one company, a coworker often finished his assignments on a timely basis, but he bashed in everyone's brains along the way. He enraged people with his lack of caring and brutal ends-justify-the-means approach. If you stepped in his way, he'd mow you down. He had no understanding of other people's priorities or time management; if you didn't get to his project right away, he'd complain to your boss or badger you into submission. "The Hammer" was a dynamic buyer, but senior management handed me the responsibility of terminating him. His intimidating style didn't cut it with his staff, the vendors or top management.

31

Every corporation has some degree of politics and buyers must finesse their way through this minefield. Some companies have rigid procedures for performance. Buyers must adhere to these methods or face a hailstorm of protest from their coworkers. Organizations have accepted ways of behaving, speaking and thinking, and circumventing the establishment is verboten. Here, the successful buyers work as a team. But all of this takes time, patience and intense planning. Does your buyer operate within the political framework, or constantly knock heads with the authorities? Your future accomplishments are riding on their political skills.

Making the Buyer Successful

Instead of standing on the sidelines, how can you improve the process for the buyer? For starters, scrutinize the buyer's face and evaluate how they're acting. Do they appear exhausted or sad? Be their friend and get them to talk about their world. Be sincere and try to help. They have ridiculous deadlines and pressures, but you do need their assistance to sell more product, and they really could benefit from your support. For example, can you or your staff handle some of the responsibility for your open projects? If you're a samurai salesperson, you'll rise to the occasion and lift a load off the buyer's shoulders, freeing them to execute the mission. If you leave the buyer decimated on the road, with tire tracks across their backs, have you done all that you could to help them to drive the business? Rise up, samurai salesperson, and do a good deed for the buyer. They will remember your assistance. As a human being, if you're able to do something nice for a business partner, shouldn't you?

If your relationship with the buyer could be categorized as difficult, or tasks aren't reaching finalization, then you need to ask yourself some questions. Were you properly prepared for the buyer during your meeting? Did you overcome all objections? Have you spoken with salespeople who are successful with this buyer and asked for their tips? Do you understand the buyer's mission and direction of their company? Are you certain that your merchandise fits with their master plan? Do you have a working relationship with the assistant buyer? Does your project rate an "A" status, or is the buyer overloaded? Have you truly helped the buyer to move this initiative forward?

Let's suppose that you are handling all the issues above superlatively, but things are still stuck in a bog? Are you dealing with THE BUYER at a headquarters location, or a buyer at a store? There's a huge difference. For example, some retail chains do have buyers—or creatures that call themselves buyers—handling purchasing on a single store basis. But they are not responsible for merchandise in the entire chain. Get to the corporate buyer.

Are you talking with the decision maker? Is the buyer empowered? The divisional merchandise manager handles the decisions in some companies, and you need to qualify that. If the buyer is new, a "kid" buyer, they might be heavily dependant on their boss to make decisions. Some people call themselves "the buyer," but, in fact, they are really the assistant buyer. Now, I was once an assistant buyer—and my buyer empowered me. I was a mighty fine assistant buyer, indeed. However, not all assistants are created equal. Make certain that, if the busy buyer hands off your stuff to their assistant, things are moving forward.

Let's suppose that you are only able to communicate with the assistant buyer, and that their boss, the buyer, is elusive and doesn't come into the office until everyone else goes home for dinner. Give up on the nagging, harassing phone calls to the buyer. They're not calling you back because they're either too busy, not terribly interested in what you're selling, or they think that your product bites the big one. It's hard to tell sometimes. After you suck down your ego and get past the humiliation, be grateful that the assistant buyer is paying attention to you. If it weren't for the assistance of assistant buyers, most of the goods on the shelves of retailers still would be sitting on warehouse shelves of manufacturers. Be thankful, very thankful, if they return your phone calls and make things happen for you. I always enjoyed receiving irate telephone calls from vendors who couldn't get to first base with my buyers. "Did you try their assistants?" I'd ask. "Well, no," stammered the supplier. There is no shame in dealing with the assistant buyer.

Now, I'm certain that various senior officers from chain stores would be launching into orbit if they heard that their buyers weren't returning calls to vendors. I've seen buyers getting chastised for not "doing their jobs." Sometimes the buyers are too buried to do their jobs. Samurai salespeople won't let themselves get caught up in this nonsense. As long as the assistant is being helpful and you see progress, be cool.

Another difficult situation for most vendors is "the buyer wants us to change the product or the packaging!" Wow, that's really awful. After all, your merchandise is so perfect that the buyer must have cloudy vision if they want to alter it. Get over yourself!! The buyer is correct 99% of the time, being on the firing line with the consumer and listening to needs of their stores. Pay attention to what they're saying. They do want to sell your product, but they need it adjusted for market conditions. They're doing you a favor.

Of course, you need to evaluate the expense for revising your goods and whether or not you want double inventory in your warehouse—the current version as well as version 2.0. If it absolutely doesn't make financial sense or the idea would violate your principles, then you need to level with the buying staff. Try to give them concrete, rational, business reasons. They may not like getting a "no" for an answer, but they should be able to appreciate your point of view. If that doesn't work, and the buyer is still climbing the walls, spewing hostile words in your direction, you might ask the divisional merchandise manager to be a tiebreaker, with the buyer's permission, naturally.

Why Be a Buyer?

You may be asking yourself, oh Samurai Sales Warriors, why on earth would anyone want to subject him or herself to such a tough existence? Why become a buyer? There are many reasons. The buying job is a rush of adrenaline. Dull days do not exist. Where else in business are you entrusted with the authority to make huge dollar-impacting decisions and where you can see the results, or sales, within a short window? You can manipulate your marketing plan and view an instant effect on business. In many cases, very young business people are given this responsibility, often handling over $100 million worth of sales volume in a year. How many careers offer that? Buyers get total departmental sales information, or a report card on their performance, every day.

One day, you build an advertisement comprised of a group of items (or *skus*, as they're called—stock keeping units, for short). When that circular or newspaper ad or TV commercial hits, and hits hard, and your stores report that customers are coming in the doors and wiping the shelves bare—that is divine. To see your hard work pay off and hundreds or thousands of pieces of merchandise go flying out the retail door—that is rewarding! Retail buyers know how well they're succeeding at their jobs, and they get a read everyday.

Why do people like being buyers? Because it is a thrilling, challenging, stimulating and highly creative and power wielding position. I thoroughly enjoyed my years as a buyer.

Chapter 5

Planning the Sales Call

As demonstrated in the preceding chapter, buyers live complicated and stress packed lives. If you don't want to be ignored, you need to approach the buyer with heavy preparation and wait for the proper time to present your products. Samurai Musashi talks about the scheduling of your opportunity.

THOUGHT # 5

From the outset you must know the applicable timing and the inapplicable timing, and from among the large and small things and the fast and slow timings find the relevant timing.... This is the main thing in strategy.[4]

Miyamoto Musashi

There is the cliché that states, "Timing is everything," and isn't that true? If you approach someone at the wrong moment, what is the likelihood of success, especially in sales? To insure that your timing is perfect, there are a series of steps you need to take leading up to the successful sales call.

In this chapter, we'll review: methods for setting up the sales call; benefits of doing your homework; preparation and confidence; the warrior attitude; and the elements of the sales presentation.

I will assume that salespeople understand how to get an appointment with a buyer. Folks have reached me via telephone, fax, email and the mail. Contacting the buyer is the part I call "is anyone at home?" If the buyer isn't receiving the signal, all your broadcasting in the world is for naught. Imagine a TV station broadcasting its message and all the televisions were turned off. You've got to connect to the buyer to get an appointment. Focus your attack. Remember, if you can't reach the buyer, who else can you speak with? Try the assistant buyer if the buyer is too busy.

Preparation

Make certain that the buyer can use your product. Prior to shooting off your communication to the buyer, you should have fully investigated the buyer's store, what products and services they offer, and how your goods will fit into the buyer's assortment. Show them how you've analyzed their needs and how your goods will fit. Are you introducing a new concept or product or line of merchandise? Let them know that when you first contact them.

If you have thoroughly done your homework, the meeting should flow smoothly. Your presentation will have direction, thereby focusing the efforts of the participants. You will not waste time having to ask questions that you should have researched before stepping into the buying office. You understand the customer's needs. Features and benefits have been incorporated into the presentation. You will have anticipated objections and mapped out how to overcome them. Preparation prior to the meeting will help you to calmly ascertain what audiovisual aids would be best to use. By preplanning, you, the samurai sales pro, will be more confident, and that will be manifested in the presentation. All of this will increase the probability of successfully closing the sale.

You need to develop your objectives prior to the meeting. What do you hope to accomplish, and what story are you trying to tell? What is the easiest way to walk the buyer through your concept? Can you deliver the message in 15 minutes or less? If you have fully prepared, using the steps below, it should be a cakewalk.

Gather information on the buyer, the merchandise on the shelves, and whatever you can glean from other suppliers. Are there specific requirements? Determine the buyers needs, short and long term. You should match these needs to the specific features and benefits of your product. Preparation can include rehearsing what you're going to say and how to say it.

Plan your use of audiovisual aids. Do you want to utilize an overhead projector or a PowerPoint presentation? Are you bringing a projector with you, or does the buyer have one? You really don't want to make your customer work for you, do you? You should bring all the tools necessary for your presentation. Then, anticipate all possible objections and how you will overcome them. You should rehearse several closes to use. If one path doesn't work for the buyer, show them your willingness and creativity by completing the sale via another route.

We've covered the different types of buying personalities you are likely to encounter. One thing in common with all buyers is that they'd prefer meeting with someone who is professional, able to answer all their questions, and is focused and confident. It is exasperating to meet with a vendor on a fact-finding mission, or one who is too timid, or unprepared because they didn't research the store or buyer. I've heard at least 100 times, "can you tell me what you're looking for because, if you do, I'm sure we could manufacture it." Buyers will think the following: "why didn't you do your research because I don't have the time to give you ideas for building

36

product. If you have finished, consumer-friendly goods, I'd be happy to review them."

Inventors regularly call buyers, sniffing around for help and direction. New vendors do the same. Please understand that once you establish a relationship with a buyer and your merchandise is on their sales floor, *then* you can brainstorm all you want. Many buyers will enjoy broadening your line or creating "line extensions" if you're stuff sells. But it is unprofessional to expect the buyer to do your job for you.

I can't emphasize enough how important it is for you to be heavily prepared and confident when you meet the buyer. I've witnessed thousands of sales presentations, and have experienced many weak, under-prepared efforts. It's not even sad to watch—it's infuriating. Don't waste the buyer's time. Realize that they may never give you another shot.

When Preparation Meets Opportunity, Success Follows

The better prepared you are for your meeting, the more likely it is that you will succeed with your objectives. There are many examples of people who practice their craft and become highly proficient. Study the history of the world's greatest artists, musicians, and businesspeople. None of them woke up one day and instantly were sensational. They trained until they were experts, having perfected their art.

Let's talk about a master of preparation and why your approach to business should mirror his technique. Tiger Woods has accomplished greatness in the world of sports. His precision with a golf club didn't miraculously appear. He is an example of preparation—he planned and prepared for success.

A good friend of mine, Bill Miller, was a top salesman in the medical supplies industry. His favorite saying is "when preparation meets opportunity, success follows." Tiger Woods is a case in point. Tiger trained ceaselessly, and his confidence reflected many years of training. This translated to a warrior's attitude accustomed to winning and achieving. Whenever Tiger was against an obstacle, he overcame it. There are stories of Tiger being mentally and physically tired, but he would work his way through the problem until he prevailed. Years of preparing gave Tiger an unlimited confidence on the golf course. He had the preparation, opportunity knocked, and success followed. Tiger performed with warrior's attitude until he won. Instead of swinging a samurai sword, his tool is a golf club. But his mental and physical preparation is on the same level as a samurai warrior. Now, many of you may spend your entire lives trying to be half as good as Tiger during your weekend golf games. Keep on trying! You also should utilize heavy preparation in the sales arena. Train to be a samurai sales warrior, with the devotion and preparation necessary to score the big order.

So you've prepared and have gotten an audience with the gatekeeper. Good for you! Let's walk through the parts of the best sales presentations I've experienced. All follow the same formula. You will walk through four parts: the opening, securing desire, handling objections and closing the sale. It'll be effortless, right? If you're properly prepared, then you are increasing your chances for success.

The Opening—Stage One

Be sure to obtain the attention and interest of the buyer, understanding that this is a critical part of your presentation. Your introduction must be original and flow naturally. Do not start out with "how's business," or "what a nice day we're having." Buyers have heard it all before, many, many times. Although these are pleasant "intros," they're terminally weak. You're about to ask this businessperson to invest thousands of dollars in your products. You can think of something more scintillating, can't you? If you start off with an original statement, you will get the buyer's interest and respect. "Why, Merrill, your fuchsia colored shirt brings out the color in your face." No, please, I'm begging you not to say that!

Unless the buyer's undivided attention and interest are secured in the first minutes of your session, you will fail. You are a samurai salesperson, acutely aware of everything going on around you. How is the buyer responding to your opening salvos? Do you have eye contact? They're focusing on you? Good. Quickly pivot into your sales presentation and Stage Two, securing desire.

Securing Desire—Stage Two

You have done your homework, so you will show the buyer how your products: fit within their assortment, enhance the sku offerings on the shelf, differentiate the buyer's store from other retailers and, most importantly, satisfy a need of consumers. Lead off with the 3 B's: benefits, benefits and benefits. If you see the buyer responding warmly, show even more stinking benefits. Are you able to incorporate a demonstration of the product or provide testimonials? Can you dramatically illustrate the strengths of this merchandise through an audio/visual display?

Launch into the various features that the product offers. Let's suppose that you were selling cordless telephones. A list of features might include: how far the signal will carry and have clarity, the ability to store your most dialed phone numbers in its memory and more. But you need to show the buyer how all these wonderful features can benefit the consumer. In this case, the customer can roam throughout their home without getting tangled up in phone cords and can easily and quickly call their friends by mashing one or two buttons. The benefits of a cordless phone simplify and enhance the consumer's experience when calling people.

At this point, the samurai salesperson needs to take stock of their environment. I call this portion of our program, "Hello? Are you aware?" Are you, the salesperson, aware of how your audience is responding? Is the buyer breathing? Are their eyes open, or is the sound of sawing logs in the background your buyer drifting off to sleep?

Here, you must ascertain that the products features and benefits are connecting with the buyer's needs. Does the buyer have any questions? Is their body language giving you non-verbal resistance? If the buyer seems disinterested, why is that? If the buyer is steadfastly following your presentation and is giving you all the positive signs of a potential commitment, try to close the sale.

Handling Objections—Stage Three

Typically, at this point in the presentation, you will move into handling objections. Remember, the buyer is paid to buy, and finding interesting new items does improve the look of their store which reflects well upon the buyer. If they're asking questions or raising objections, that's good. It gives you an opportunity to interact and help them to evaluate the merchandise. You're calm because you thoroughly prepared for the objections. Walk through them one by one and don't leave any objections unanswered. If the buyer seems comfortable with your explanations, close the sale.

Closing the Sale—Stage Four

Opportunities for closing may occur throughout the opening, or during the securing desire and handling objections phases. A samurai salesperson is always ready to close the sale. You are prepared, the opportunity arises— close the sale. Some buyers might write you a purchase order at this point. The greater likelihood is that larger retailers will require information to enter your product into their computer system: cost of the item, dimensions, order quantities and more. Experienced salespeople know that if the item isn't "set up in the system," buyers won't be able to order it, and you won't get paid. Don't plan on walking out the door with a million dollar order—it's not probable. But you can get a commitment.

Let's talk about the commitment. Is it verbal or have they sent you an email or letter indicating their interest? If your product will be in limited distribution initially, tell the buyer that you need purchase orders to hold their goods. Fifteen years ago, I often gave verbal or even handwritten projections to vendors. In recent years, I always gave suppliers a commitment in writing, and I recommend that you require it as well. I have seen many manufacturers suffer as a result of a projection that never materialized into a bona fide purchase order. Even if you've known the buyer for ten years, get the purchase order. Suppose that the buyer's commitment doesn't metamorphosize into a legal order. Suppose you built a boatload of merchandise and it's sitting on your warehouse shelves. What are you going to do? It's interesting that suppliers in the Orient will thank you for projections, but won't start ordering raw materials to build the actual products until they receive a firm purchase order. Why is that? Even with a great relationship, a projection can be worthless. For your protection, get a stinking order.

Chapter 6

How Does a Buyer Look at Things? (Part 1 of an incredibly long download) Assortments and Financials

I maintain that the strength of a samurai salesperson comes from deep knowledge of your customer, the buyer. Do you remember the statement: **"Think like a merchant or forever act like a peddler?"** If you fully comprehend how a buyer thinks and strategizes, you will be infinitely more successful with them.

THOUGHT #6

You can become a master of strategy by training alone with a sword, so that you can understand the enemy's stratagems, his strength and resources, and come to appreciate how to apply strategy to beat ten thousand enemies.[5]

Miyamoto Musashi

Two key parts of a buyer's business strategy are assortments and financials. The assortment is the products offered for sale on the store's shelves. Financials include budgeting and retail math.

First, let's examine how a buyer looks at their assortment and how they pick merchandise? The process starts with an impressive sales meeting between the buyer and you, the samurai sales warrior. You've shown your products to the buyer and now they are evaluating them. What are some of the thoughts drifting around in the buyer's mind? Please, keep your sarcastic comments about "things drifting around in the buyer's minds" to yourself.

The buyer is entrusted with purchasing merchandise that will fit within a store's point of view. I call the buyer "the gatekeeper" because they can open or close the door depending on who is trying to enter. If the store is selling office supplies and you sell pantyhose, the gatekeeper is likely to keep you out. Now, being a clever salesperson, you might say, "well, women buy office supplies and they need pantyhose. You will be taking special care of your customer by offering my products."

The situation mentioned above actually took place years ago. The CEO of a major office supply retailer discovered that his buyer was going to add pantyhose to their assortment. If his store was a mass merchant, like Target or Wal-Mart, then pantyhose and office supplies belonged in the assortment. However, the CEO ran a store that focused on office supplies only. I

41

remember what the CEO said to his buyer: "You can add pantyhose to this store when my dead, rotten, stinking corpse is in the ground." The end of the story is that they never added the pantyhose.

Here's the point—a buyer will add your merchandise to the assortment as long as it fits within the store's direction and point of view. You need to walk through the buyer's store and fully comprehend their focus. Don't think that you will be able to alter the way a retailer goes to market.

Brand names and Private Label

Many retailers in America devoutly support branded merchandise and for very good reasons. A brand is built over time and is synonymous with quality. If you examine some of the most famous brands today, their products are considered to be great quality, offering superior attributes vs. their competition. What images are created in your mind when you hear the names Sony, Panasonic, 3M, AT&T, IBM, and Coca Cola? It's easier for the consumer to buy a product if they recognize the brand. Therefore, if you manufacture merchandise that has a famous name, you typically will find chain store buyers that want to purchase your products. Department, specialty, warehouse club, mass market and superstores all feature branded goods.

These stores also do a fine job of developing their own store brands, or private label merchandise. Store brands can be attractively packaged and offer features and benefits that are similar to the major name branded goods, but at a much lower price. Compare Listerine mouthwash and the various private label knock offs available at drugstores and supermarkets. Buyers negotiate with smaller manufacturers that can produce essentially the same type of product as the brand, but the private label factory doesn't have the brand's overhead (advertising, salespeople, etc.). Consequently, they can sell private label goods at lower costs to the chain store buyer and, in turn, create lower retail prices for the consumer.

Retail buyers are weighing the pros and cons of building their brand name assortments, while balancing the opportunities for store brands. Any store that represents quality merchandise must include some brand name goods in their product assortment. However, the consumer might prefer to save money, by forgoing the status of branded goods. Private label merchandise can fill that need.

Branded and private label goods are one more consideration that the buyer needs to make when they are building their product assortments. Of course, if you offer a well-made product without a significant "name," buyers will be interested too.

Good, Better, Best

Any well-designed product assortment will include good, better and best merchandise. For example, you can find a "good" DVD player for $99—$129 that has limited features—it will play your discs and offers a decent quality image on your television. That is an entry-level price point. Midrange, or "better," DVD machines can sell for $150 to $300, providing enhanced picture quality and various features. DVD players rise from $300 and climb into thousands of dollars at the high end ("best"). Supposedly, these products are state of the art, giving the videophile an unsurpassed image.

Depending on the retail store's point of view, they can offer good, better and best merchandise to the consumer. Some retailers, like department stores, are known to offer merchandise in the mid to upper price ranges, and you wouldn't find "good" merchandise with low retails. Consumer electronics chain stores often provide entry level to mid range priced goods (good and better items). If you were shopping for the "best" in electronics, you might have to go to a high-end specialty store.

Similarly, you can find private label products covering good, better and best price points. For example, during my office products days, I sold store brand merchandise at "good" entry-level prices—legal pads with thin cardboard backing. This was priced below the "good" products from national name brand manufacturers. For the "better" and "best" legal pads, I provided name brand goods with heavier cardboard backs and thicker and smoother paper. I offered merchandise that would satisfy any consumer. In the pet industry, the approach was different with the store brand. Here, my store chose to sell private label merchandise that was equal to or superior to the best name brand goods in the market. The retailer's focus on good, better and best merchandise can vary from store to store, and the management of the retailer preplans this. The buyer is evaluating where your products will fit in the good, better, best spectrum.

While building the assortment, the buyer is looking at other factors. Before, during and after a sales presentation, the buyer is thinking if your products have the right design and color, and will it fit on the shelf with the other skus? Fitting on the shelf means both physically fitting onto the surface of the shelf and fitting within the point of view of the store. Department stores stand for better quality apparel—are you offering that type of product to that store's buyer?

Does the buyer already have a similar product in their assortment? If so, did you know that and how will you handle that objection? The buyer evaluates if the item is appropriate for the entire national assortment (put into all stores), or if it's a regionally specific product. Most chain stores have A/B/C stores. This can mean large (A), medium (B), and small (C) square foot stores, or it can designate large, medium or small volume locations. If your item is very expensive and has a limited appeal to the broad cross-section of humanity that enters the buyer's store, it would not sell in all their sites. Some products are only appropriate for select markets.

Basic, Promotional or Cutting Edge

Is your product basic or promotional or cutting edge? The buyer is sizing up your merchandise because their approach to marketing the product will depend on how it is classified. If you've thought this through, you will be more effective in selling the buyer. If goods are basic, they are like socks, or underwear, or file folders, or spatulas. The customer usually will buy them when they need them, and advertising them at a hot price might not get the consumer running into your store. Will you rush to the retailer to get a $5 sock for $3.99? A basic item is nice to have, makes an assortment complete and a buyer must offer them.

Promotional merchandise moves rapidly when offered in an ad at a sale price. Good examples are most consumer electronics, food and motor oil. If filet mignon steak normally sells for $12 a pound and a store offers it for $7 a pound, expect higher sales volume. Televisions will fly off the shelves if the retailer offers a significant discount.

Cutting edge goods attract avant-garde customers—folks that like to be first. When CD players first came out in 1984, they were selling for $1,500 and more. Only the customers who demanded the latest technology first came to the stores. As the price dropped below $500, unit movement started its ascent. Today, you can buy portable CD players well under $100, and they have become mass-market items, in most homes throughout America. Cutting edge goods are nice to advertise because they establish your store as advanced, offering the latest and greatest products available. They help the retailer to differentiate their store from others.

Where do your products belong—in the basic, promotional or cutting edge category? You will need to have a different approach when you try to sell the buyer on the merits of these goods. If you have promotional merchandise and offer the retailer extra advertising funds, you're going in the right direction. Basic merchandise can have other incentives attached to their purchase, whether it is an increased rebate, or advertising (coop) program, or special times of the year that you can buy them at lower prices. For cutting edge goods, the retailer wants to be first to market—can you promise them that?

When merchandise is extremely new, cutting edge, a novel concept, have you backed this product introduction with funds sufficient to alert the

44

marketplace to its existence? Revolutionary products require more detailed marketing plans than other goods. You must have a well-defined advertising plan in trade and consumer publications. Television commercials and newspaper ads can be employed. You should partner with the retail buyer to segue way into their ad plans as well.

During my career, smaller manufacturers with wonderful new products and no marketing plans often approached me. They'd rely on me to do all the promoting of the merchandise. I'd explain to them that a major new product introduction into the marketplace was a "pioneering effort." Just as the pioneers crossed America and encountered harsh conditions as they established their new homesteads, a pioneering effort with a new item can require extra expenditures of time and money to notify the public and establish the item's place in an assortment. If the vendor hasn't thought out all the details on a new item launch, the buyer could be reluctant to carrying the merchandise.

Differentiation

What else is the buyer contemplating? By adding your goods to a store's assortment, will this differentiate, or set their store apart from all other retailers? If a store is one of the few places you can find certain merchandise, that will pull customers to them, thereby differentiating them from other stores. Customers shop for merchandise that satisfies their needs. If one store regularly stocks products that meet those desires, the consumer will frequent that retailer. The merchandise content or assortment differs between retail chains. If your wares enhance the look of the store, and that attracts more shoppers, the buyer will purchase more from you. This is critically important to buyers.

Another part of the evaluation process going on in the buyer's head is whether you are the right vendor for their store. A department store or specialty store buyer is looking for quality merchandise at fair prices, delivered on a timely basis. Can you provide that? Discount and mass market stores want all of that but at a hot price—some of those stores will settle for a little less quality if they can get a much lower price. All buyers utilize standards to judge your performance and how well you meet their needs, and we'll talk more about that later on.

45

Retail Prices and Profit Margins

The buyer is considering if your item has an invoice cost that will permit a selling price high enough to generate a profit, yet move quantity. Will the profit margin fit within the buyer's budgeted margin goals? You need to understand the requirements for each store you sell. Let's suppose that your item is similar to a product offered by another manufacturer. Yes, I understand that your product is superior. In this example, most of the retailers offering the other guy's product have established $9.99 as the hot retail price. If you sell your merchandise to the buyer for $7.25 and the buyer's margin plan is 50%, it doesn't work. The buyer's retail selling price would be nearly $11 at a 50% margin. Either the buyer will have to accept a lower margin for this item to hit $9.99, or induce you to sell at a lower cost so they can hit the competitive price.

When I was a buyer, one of my favorite discussions with vendors involved the "If you, Mr. Buyer, sell an item at a lower price, you will move more units and grow your profits" debate. If a product is offered for sale at a price lower than the buyer's margin plan, can you drive more units to make up for the loss in margin? Many vendors I've met have insisted that lower prices will move additional units, thereby dropping more profit dollars into the bottom line.

Let's examine this concept closely. Using the previous example of the $9.99 price, with a $5.00 cost instead, every retail sale will generate $4.99 in profit, a 50% margin (50% of the selling price is profit). If we sold 1,000 pieces, the profit would be $4,990 on retail sales of $9,990. By dropping the retail price to $7.99, would we move more units? That's the first question you need to ask yourself. For the sake of this exercise, let's presume that you'd move 20% more product, or 1,200 total units. But in this scenario, the profit per unit has dropped to $2.99.

Do the math: 1,200 times $2.99 profit for each, equals $3,588, on retail sales of $11,988. The profit decreased by $1,402 and the retail sales increased by $1,998. So, even though the sales through the cash register went up, the profit dollars went down. Also, the margin percent dropped to 37.4%, a decrease of -12.6%.

Let's try this problem another way. If dropping the retail price to $7.99 was extremely exciting to the consumer, this was a highly recognized best selling item, the price had never been advertised below $9.99 and the result would be a 100% increase in unit movement, that would be better. Here's why: Increasing the original unit plan of 1,000 pieces by a 100% increase would throw off 2,000 pieces sold. The profit dollars per item remain the same at $2.99. Now try the math: $2.99 times 2,000 units equals $5,980—a growth of $990 profit over the first example. Retail sales go up as well—

2,000 times $7.99 equals $15,980, a lift of $5,990 dollars through the cash register over the first example.

There are many ways that you can interpret the results above. You can say that more customers were brought into the store and it drove greater retail sales. Some of those additional customers may have purchased additional items that helped the overall store's business. More profit dollars were created. That's good. However, the margin percent is still 37.4%, well below the buyer's plan. If you sold too many goods at 37.4%, it would eventually erode the buyer's profit percent.

Unless you are fully prepared for this argument, that lowering retail prices will dramatically improve profits, I'd stay away from it. You must mathematically prove that this can work, or put money where your mouth is. I've seen buyers force commitments from their supplier to guarantee the profit if they were to sell at a lower margin percent. Can you really guarantee the number of units that will be sold? What if you miss? Are you willing to cover the lost margin dollars? If not, don't push it.

Competition

How does the buyer assess your merchandise offering vs. their competition? Your products must improve the look of their store, help to differentiate them from the competition and fill a need in the market. Buyers call new products that replicate existing merchandise "me-too." Being the same or looking the same as other vendor's goods won't score points for the buyer. If your products are me-too, you can't help to differentiate the buyer's store from the competition. Sometimes buyers will purchase a similar item from a different vendor so the packaging and item will appear to be different from what is offered across the street at their competition.

The buyer is considering whether your products can compete with similar goods at their competition. Will the price the buyer needs to charge to be competitive still throw off enough profit? Are you charging too much, and the buyer won't be able to be competitive?

Many retailers today operate with price zones, adjusting their retails based on local market conditions. Should one crazy competitor choose to sell specific items at cost in Chicago, the competitive stores in that town could match the price. However, the rest of the retail chain could be at higher prices.

The buyer is wondering if your items will be carried by their competition and bashed into the ground (prices dropped to an amazingly low level). Are you sharply priced vs. *your* competition? If you are selling the buyer's competition, are you charging the same cost?

47

Buyers have nightmares. One of them goes like this: they open the Sunday newspaper and find out that their competition is buying the same merchandise from you and selling it for dollars less. It's in print, so everyone, including the buyer's management can witness the problem. They will presume that you gave a better price to the competition. Good luck on convincing them otherwise.

Another nightmare has the buyer negotiating with you and getting some items on an exclusive arrangement. This nightmare begins when the buyer walks into his biggest competitor and finds these exclusive goods on their selling floor.

Another nightmare involves your competition—you fail to keep up with them. A buyer selects your merchandise because you were first to the market. By jumping on your merchandise and supporting it, the buyer's store looks cutting edge to the consumer. This differentiates the buyer's store from all others. A few months pass and your competition "knocks you off," creating their version of your product, and it appears in a store that competes with your buyer. In this case, the buyer has a nightmare because they believed that you would help their store stay ahead of their competition and you didn't.

I've had many nightmares during my years in the buying office. In many cases, the manufacturers cleverly assessed the damage and helped to turn the bad situation around. There are many nice solutions to the above problems. You can invest more heavily in the retailer through increased advertising; you can offer a price reduction; you can get the buyer the first run of another major product. But, for heaven's sake, do something to appease the buyer. When nightmares occur, the buyer comes across like an idiot to their management. If you understand politics, you don't want your buyer to have their image tarnished. You need them on your side. Take care of them!

Point of Purchase Materials and Training

In addition to the above thoughts, the buyer is wondering if you have provided adequate signing or point of purchase (POP) materials. Will you help the buyer to sell these products? Although some retailers have taken the responsibility on themselves for proper signing, a few stores don't have the resources or time or money to do so. If your new item presentation includes signing that you will create to their specifications, you will please the buyer. Or, do you have a team that can develop great POP with the store's design crew? Remember the buyer's time crunch. By having a sign package available that the buyer doesn't need to develop, you'll be assuring a higher likelihood of success for your products.

How will the buyer teach store associates about your new item? Especially with the larger retail chains, this is a complication. As a store gets larger, it is more difficult to communicate and train store personnel about products. Some chains have trainers out in the field, but many stores do not have that luxury. Information is largely communicated via websites, emails or printed sheets. Just as one group of store associates is trained, factor in turnover and you have another concern for the buyer. If you are able to assist the buyer, by getting your field personnel out to the retailer's stores for training, that's a plus. Can your team help the retailer to put up your POP? Can you support the retailer's field trainers? Can you assist the buyer with the writing of the memo to the store organization? These are thoughts going through the buyer's mind. If you anticipate these issues, you will be way ahead of the game.

So, the buyer is examining many things prior to purchasing your merchandise. Does the product fit into their assortment and does the vendor meet the needs of the store? What is the buyer's competition doing with similar items? Also, the buyer has to consider local markets and their special demands.

Ad Funds and New Items

Do you have advertising monies earmarked for these products? In my lifetime, I've experienced savvy vendors who offered extra funds to alert the consumer about their new products. Also, there have been arrogant and ignorant manufacturers who didn't understand the need for new item ad funds. They should never have walked into my office. Make the sale easy for the buyer and give them all the support they require to move your merchandise. If you're not offering an ad package with your goods, how will the buyer market the products? Should the buyers be clever enough to dip into their own "slush-fund" of advertising funds? Dream on, samurai. Buyers rarely have that kind of cash stashed away. If you're dealing with hard goods buyers, as they say in New York, "fuggeddaboudit" (forget about it). Hard goods buyers never have enough money to run their ads.

There are three types of new item introductions. One, when you're a totally new vendor and all your products are unfamiliar to a store. Two, when you are regularly selling to a retailer and you're adding another item to your assortment. This could be called a line extension—you offer a 2" and 4" rawhide bone and wish to add a 6" bone. Three, you are introducing a new line of products, never available before. This typically is a revolutionary product. The introduction of the CD, DVD, non-stick cookware, and cat food that prevented hairballs all were considered major new item launches. Yes, even anti-hairball food was major—do you want your cat to "yack" all over your rug?

In scenario one and three, telling the consumer that your goods are now on the shelves could drive significant sales. In a line extension, it is rare to advertise. However, the point of the story is: make it easy for the buyer, give them advertising money when needed, and close the sale.

Inventory Support

There are other things on the buyer's minds before they give you the go ahead to ship the goods. Is there open to buy for this? Does the store have money allocated to buy this product? What if item doesn't sell? If the vendor's inventory is replacing merchandise currently on the shelf, will the new vendor take back the old manufacturer's products? Let's discuss each of these.

In some retail chains, rigid inventory budgets are maintained, and this is called "open to buy." When I was a department store buyer, open to buy dictated if we were able to purchase merchandise or not. Essentially, the buyers are given monthly inventory goals to hit. If their inventory climbs above that level, open to buy forbids additional spending—you can't buy. Learn if your buyer has to deal with such a system, because if they're overspent, they're not writing purchase orders to you.

What if an item doesn't sell? This question is usually on a buyer's mind. Will the vendor support a return or mark down if the goods don't move? Now, I wouldn't purchase an item if I doubted that it would sell. However, some buyers like to have a "guaranteed sale" arranged with the manufacturer before they buy new goods. In this agreement, the vendor has given a verbal or written promise to take goods back that don't sell. My advice to the buyer and seller is to get this offer in writing because people do become forgetful. Surprisingly, this isn't the best deal for the buyer. One, you shouldn't buy something if you aren't comfortable that it will sell. Two, if it's a new vendor and the merchandise dies on the vine, if you ship the goods back, the vendor owes you money. You can whistle "Dixie" before some vendors pay you if you're not regularly doing business with them. It's always amazed me how many vendors offer a guaranteed sale on their products; many vendors failed to cut a check back to my company when the product died a miserable death. I've known too many buyers who were left with cruddy merchandise and no way out—on a guaranteed sale. Instead, what I've recommended to buyers and sellers is for the buyer to put the merchandise invoice "on hold" with the accounting department. This way, the goods haven't been paid for. Under these circumstances, the buyer does have the ability to ship goods back without incurring a debit, or negative, balance on their accounting books.

Another way out, or method to calm the buyer's fears, is to offer markdown money. This works if you're an existing vendor with a quality relationship. Here, the buyer sells the goods in their stores at reduced retails without incurring additional handling charges for packing goods up for a return. It's interesting that there are two points of view on whether to return poor sellers back to the vendor or to mark them down. One group of merchants believes that the best thing to do with horrible goods is to get them quickly out of the store, thereby freeing up valuable shelf space for new saleable merchandise. Another group of retailers prefers to mark goods down and capture some sales from distressed merchandise. In both scenarios, the store operations folk get hit with handling expenses. Either the stores spend labor hours boxing up goods, or they have to set these goods up in another area of the store. How do I prefer to go? If the merchandise really is "howling," a dog supreme, then I'd prefer to ship the "howler" back to the vendor. On the other hand, if the products are selling, but not quickly, I'd juice the sales by cutting the price dramatically—at least 50% for starters— provided the vendor is funding the markdown. Regardless, whether you agree to funding a markdown or accepting a return on slow selling goods, put the arrangement into writing.

Lastly, there is this scenario: "If the vendor's inventory is replacing merchandise currently on the shelf, will the new vendor take back the old manufacturer's products?" In the more sophisticated industries, most vendors are accustomed to this entry fee. To clear the shelf, making way for a new vendor's merchandise, they buy up all the old vendor's products. Now, I've had manufacturers become incensed when I offered this plan to them. "You're kidding me, right?" one vendor said to me. "Why should I take back someone else's products? If you want to buy my products, can't you liquidate the old stuff?" Nope. Remember, it's a new day and age.

Buyers today expect you to offer this type of assistance. If you are a small manufacturer and you plan on doing business with a "big box" retailer, get ready for this expectation. Here's the justification: If you are taking over the space from another factory, it's probably because the goods don't sell well or there's some other issue. The retailer wants the old vendor and any attached problems to go away quickly and painlessly. Marking down products isn't totally effective. Some of the buyer's higher traffic stores will quickly move through the inventory, while the smaller stores might own these products forever. If you take back the goods, theoretically, they will leave the building immediately (provided all the stores have the same sense of urgency as the buyer). Nice and clean, no muss, no fuss, you lift the bad vendor's boatload of crud and substitute your beautiful, shining, fresh, new products. That makes buyers happy. It also reduces any competition on the shelves between the old vendor's goods and your stuff.

Where should you go with someone else's merchandise? Frankly, the buyer probably doesn't care as long as the goods go away. Today, manufacturers ship undesirables to other countries, frequently to Mexico or South America. With the growth of businesses online, there are websites catering to closeout goods as well. Other sites feature merchandise auctions. Jobbers throughout America are available to purchase various products at deep discounts, often pennies on the dollar. Yes, I know it hurts you when you buy goods that aren't yours, stuff you really don't want, and the buyer bills you for its full value, and then you have to practically throw it away or write it off. Business can be brutal. But don't think about the short-term impact on your finances—consider the long-term gain.

So, buyers have multiple considerations before they add your products to their assortments. Remember that buyers have limited time to do their jobs and they're normally too busy to tell you everything they need. You should have discovered that during your research of the retailer. You should be an expert on your products and the potential needs of your customer. Be prepared for all the issues mentioned above and you might have a chance to get your skus into more stores.

Financial Budgets

Of course, there are many aspects of retail buying that occur far from the watchful eyes of samurai salespeople. Buyers do have functions that are uniquely theirs. Some of these involve retail budgeting and financial analysis. By understanding how buyers budget and analyze their financial information, you will comprehend how your products fit into the big picture.

The budgets that retailers create are sales, inventory and profit plans to guide their business in the coming year. Also, they utilize these numbers to compare to their actual performance. The budgets are roadmaps that retailers follow. Are they "hitting the budget," "on the budget," "missing plan," or "exceeding the budget?" If they are increasing sales by 8%, but the plan was to grow by +12%, there won't be any happy faces. If last year's profit margin was 54.57%, and this year's budget states 55.35%, but the actual margin percent is coming in at 55.58%—happy days.

Behind the scenes, buyers build financial budgets for their areas of responsibility, called *departments*. Prior to the beginning of the new fiscal year, buyers, merchandise managers, vice presidents, inventory managers, store management and members of the finance department start creating the financial goals. This process starts out very scientific, with all folks involved reviewing performances from past years. Did a department post an increase during certain seasonal periods? What were the best and worst months for this merchandise? Have there been many years of growth? How will competition affect this area next year? Are there going to be new, revolutionary products that can drive sales in this category? Or is this area on a downward slide, due to lackluster merchandise? Perhaps, the retailer is unhappy with the profitability of this merchandise and is downsizing the assortment—that impacts the sales budget, too.

Departments are split into subcategories, typically called classes or subclasses, and the process is the same for these smaller sales areas as well. A budget is built for the component parts of the department and adds up to the total department's sales plan. A large department might be called "consumer electronics," but each subclass might include televisions, telephones, DVD players and cell phones. Add up the sales plans for the subclasses, and you get the buyer's total departmental plan.

What information can be gleaned from the sales history of these classes, and how can it be applied to a financial prognostication for the following year? The numbers can reveal past and future trends. Also, by layering on top of that information what is happening to this category in the marketplace—the impact of new goods, manufacturers jockeying for position, retail competition placing an emphasis on a department—it can be forecast how high or low the budgeted numbers need to be. All of the information merges to create a picture. Does the buyer have a healthy, thriving business? Will the vendor community help to maintain consumer interest and retail sales through the introduction of hot, new products?

How does that impact you, great samurai salesperson? For starters, if your goods are lumped into a down trending department, is the retailer going to fund inventory at previous levels? Doubtful. They will build a budget for the future in which sales and inventory is lowered. If your buyer has designed a plan to dynamically promote a category, their sales plan will boom, and so will your purchase orders. You need to have an understanding of what direction the buyer is planning for their areas of responsibility and how you can help them to achieve the financial plan. Similarly, if your company's budget details movement of tremendous amounts of goods and you don't communicate that to the buyer, how can you expect the buyer to help you to sell the merchandise? We're talking about planning and driving a business forward, and the salesperson and retail buyer must be in sync.

Financial Analysis

We've discussed the budgeting process and now need to delve into financial analysis. Why do buyers analyze the financial performance of their areas? It should be obvious. As you drive your car along a roadway, you are headed towards a goal, a destination. If you're leaving Atlanta, Ga., going to Savannah, you will watch the signs along the way, judging your distance from your target. You'll notice the environment as you travel, making adjustments for traffic, monitoring your speed as required for a timely arrival. The further you are from Atlanta, the less familiar the surroundings become, and your driving becomes more cautious. A restaurant might beckon to you, and you could stop there to pause, evaluate the progress of your trip and ready yourself for the remainder of the journey. You may notice unusual things in route—other drivers on the roadway who are dangerous and need to be avoided. Or you could encounter rough terrain that requires a more careful approach to circumvent an accident. Thoughts on your mind might include how pleasant it will be to see friends and family when you reach your objective.

Correspondingly, financial analysis is a critical part of a retailer's world. Buyers are aimed in a direction and shoot towards a sales and profit goal. They need to monitor their progress along the way and make adjustments to their business if the results, or financial numbers, are not indicating sufficient progress. Competition could be heavier than normal, or the consumer may have lost their interest in a product category. Buyers must pause from their hectic schedules and analyze the information, draw a conclusion and develop a strategy for continued forward movement. Sometimes, business conditions throw you into a downward spiral and a serious course correction is required—immediate surgery must be performed or market share will be lost. Obstacles to hitting the plan are reviewed and challenged. A buyer's annual salary review, or bonus, in some cases, is based on hitting their financial objectives. I can assure you that buyers are thinking about how pleasant it will be to reach these goals.

Many retail chains provide daily sales and margin information for their buying teams. Typically, a buyer can view departmental sales, sales increases or decreases, and margin percents. All numbers are compared to the previous year's achievements. Are the department's financials continuing to climb? Are the advertisements pulling people into the stores and encouraging them to buy the products? Did the buyer's competition run a major advertised sale event and damage the results for that time period? You can learn a lot from examining the numbers. If they are missing the sales plan in a department, you can be assured that some member of management is having a conversation with the buyer. More likely, the buyer has seen the trend and is taking action to correct the situation.

Margin Percent

Finally, the buyer compares the margin percent from the previous year to the current year. Are the departments tracking based on the forecast?

Initial margin percent is calculated as follows: **Retail minus invoice cost, divided by retail.**

Take the retail price of the merchandise and deduct the invoice cost of the goods. Divide that number by the retail price to get the margin percent.

Let's put numbers into this exercise: An item retails for $50. Deduct the cost, $20, and you get $30. Divide $30 by the retail price ($50) and you get 60% initial margin.

Essentially, what this computation tells the buyer is that 60% of the $50 retail price is profit. In the example above, $30 is the profit, and $30 is 60% of $50. The margin dollars are $30, money made on the sale of that item.

If the item above continues to sell for $50, but the margin percent drops—the vendor raises the price of this sku to $25 (formerly $20)—the margin percent drops to 50% (formerly 60%). Now, the margin dollars generated from the sale of this item are reduced to $25 (formerly $30).

Salespeople and buyers often get into a discussion over what is more important—the margin % or the margin dollars? Although you take margin dollars to the bank, many buyers are fixated on margin percent. Most buyers in America get a daily report of their previous days sales and margin percent. Yet, many corporate cultures review the margin dollars only at year-end. Although they should be paying attention to the margin dollars, most buyers are focused on margin percent. Try to fight that one—it's ingrained in their brains.

You must ascertain how a buyer analyzes their business. Do they pursue margin percent or margin dollars? Here's why: If you *suggest* to the buyer that they try a lower retail on one of your items to excite the consumer, it will generate a lower margin percent as well. That won't thrill the buyer. "But, you will bring in more customers to buy this product, and that increase in unit sales will drive higher margin dollars," you might say. Remember, we've covered this line of reasoning earlier in this chapter. If the buyer is fixated on a margin percent, and your merchandise is dragging that percent down, woe is you.

Unless you are prepared to show the buyer how they can drive more margin dollars, help them to achieve a respectable margin percent. If you hit the sales numbers and hit the margin objective, you will generate the needed margin dollars. Sales people who don't respect a buyer's margin plan, may not get to first base with the buyer.

GMROI and Inventory Turnover

You need to be familiarized with two other extremely important calculations that buyers utilize: GMROI and inventory turnover. Both of these tools evaluate the performance of their inventory investment.

GMROI stands for *gross margin return on investment*. For every one dollar invested, what is the return?

Turn or Turnover means *the number of times that the retailer sells their inventory during the course of the year*. Let's walk through inventory turn first.

Turnover is calculated as follows: **annual sales at cost divided by annual average inventory at cost.**

Suppose that a category produced annual sales at cost of $10,000 and the buyer carried an average monthly inventory of $1,000 at cost. That means their department had various inventory levels over 12 months that averaged $1,000 per month. Take the annual sales of $10,000 and divide it by the average monthly inventory of $1,000. That equals an inventory turn of 10 times—not bad. For the buyer's average monthly inventory investment of $1,000, they returned sales 10 times that amount. Or you can say that the buyer took the $1,000 monthly investment in inventory and resold that inventory 10 times.

The higher the turnover number, the better the management of the inventory. However, if the turnover number is too high, there may not be enough inventory in the stores. Let's alter the example above. If the average monthly inventory was $750 and the annual sales remained the same: annual sales of $10,000 divided by $750 would equal a turn of 13.3. Less inventory is driving the same sales. Theoretically, the lower inventory is more productive. However, maybe $750 worth of monthly inventory makes the store shelves look bare. It's a balancing act that all retailers perform. How do you squeeze the best results from your assets without looking like your stores are out of merchandise.

The reverse can be true, if the turn number is too low—there is probably too much inventory. Utilizing the example, if sales stay at $10,000, but the average monthly inventory number rises to $2,000, the turn drops to 5 times. In this case, there might be so much merchandise that the store has to stockpile it in their backroom storage areas.

"How does this impact me," the samurai salespeople are asking. "I didn't force the buyer to buy the number of units they chose. They did their weird-ass calculations and placed the orders. No guns were pointed at the buyer's heads." Great, wonderful point of view, isn't it? I've actually heard those words several times during my career. They're sensitive, yet subtly uncaring, don't you think?

Turnover does impact your business. If a buyer is sitting on too much inventory and their turn is horrible, they won't be placing purchase orders. They won't need your goods for a while. However, if the stores regularly look like an army invaded them and bought everything in site, then the turn is flying through the roof, and the buyer or inventory manager needs to get more goods, pronto. Are you prepared for the orders? Did you notice that the store was wiped out of product? Have you communicated any of this to your manufacturing department?

GMROI

Now that you understand the impact of inventory turnover on your business, let's examine another financial tool. **Gross Margin Return On Investment** is abbreviated **GMROI**, and is pronounced like "Jim-Roy." Its computation employs the turnover ratio and adds one more bit of math.

GMROI: Take the annual sales at cost and divide it by the annual average inventory at cost (calculation for turnover), then multiply that number times the Gross Profit %.

Now, some of the more astute mathematical wizards out there will be quick to point out that they have utilized other methods to calculate GMROI. Yes, there are a few ways. I experienced the formula presented here in several major national retail chains.

In the example, we had annual sales of $10,000 and divided it by an average monthly inventory of $1,000, arriving at the number 10. The gross profit % of the category is 55%. Multiply 10 X .55 = $5.50. For every dollar you invested, it returned $5.50, a pretty good return.

Some folks like expressing the result in a different way—as a percent. The annual sales of $10,000 are still divided by average inventory of $1,000 = 10. Then, multiply 10 X 55 = 550%. In this example, for every dollar invested, you achieved a 550% return.

Either way you slice it or analyze it, GMROI is a computation being heavily utilized by today's buyers. Here's why: let's suppose that you achieve great sales off a promotion, but your inventory investment is very high. How will that impact the GMROI? Using the problem above, if the sales remain at $10,000, but the average inventory climbs to $1,250 (there was a lot more inventory left on the shelf following the sale than planned), how do the numbers change? Take $10,000 and divide it by $1,250 = 8. Then multiply 8 times .55 = $4.40. Or, you can multiply 8 times 55 = 440%. Regardless, the original GMROI has dropped.

The point here is that too much inventory can damage the GMROI results. Sales can be great, but pile on the inventory and you've weakened the "Jim-Roy." Many buyers, myself included, have overbought for a promotion and been hung with goods for months. Twenty years ago, buyers cared about sales and let the accountants worry about too much inventory. Drive the business, full speed ahead!! In today's climate, buyers are tied to their inventory management teams and are responsible for achieving the corporation's inventory goals.

"How's this impact me," you ask. One of my pet peeves from years of retailing is that salespeople don't always question the buyer about how their merchandise is selling. They should ask for detail, but most don't. Your sales might be good, but your retailer could be dying from too much inventory. Their turn and GMROI might be way below expectations. That will impact their future purchases from you, and it also colors their point of view towards your products. You could have great sales, but a doubt has been placed in the buyer's mind about the viability of your products. Now, a wise, retail samurai merchant will see the big picture and adjust future purchases to more intelligent levels. But you won't always deal with sophistication and intelligence. There is nothing wrong with you questioning the size of a purchase, or having your inventory folks talking with the retailer's inventory management.

If you fully comprehend how your buyer is analyzing your business, you can respond accordingly. A wise vendor will help a buyer to move through extra inventory by funding additional advertising or a temporary retail markdown. Buyers are usually appreciative of all the assistance they can get. It means that you truly are a partner in business with them, that you care about positive financial results and you are there to support them.

Chapter 7

"I can't get the buyer to buy!" Overcoming Objections.

THOUGHT #7

Because you can win quickly by taking the lead, it is one of the most important things in strategy. There are several things involved in taking the lead. You must make the best of the situation, see through the enemy's spirit so that you grasp his strategy and defeat him.[6]

Miyamoto Musashi

The successful samurai salesperson is looking around them, analyzing their environment, taking stock of movement from their competition, seeing the buyer's point of view, and making adjustments to their plans as a result. A warrior salesperson has to be in first place. You want to be at the top of the buyer's mind, the best at your profession, representing the finest products. Mushashi talks about taking the lead position in battle, and there are many famous sayings out there covering this topic. You've all heard, "lead, follow or get out of the way." One of my favorites is: "Unless you're the lead dog, the view never changes." You really don't want to follow the hindquarters of other sales people, do you? Part of being the alpha dog, the lead animal in the pack, requires you to deal with complications— overcoming a buyer's resistance to completing the sale.

Let me give you some of my reasons for being unwilling to buy from a salesperson. It might have been *timing*, that the salesperson caught me during a difficult period. Perhaps, my boss had made an impossible request, or I had been working too many hours and was tired. My team could have encountered problems in completing our duties: advertised goods were running late or hadn't shipped, or a critical sale sign hadn't been printed, or someone hadn't followed through on their promise to complete an assignment.

If the timing appears to be undesirable, get to your point quickly, or ask the buyer to reschedule, if possible.

Often, a salesperson lost me in the first few minutes of their introduction because they *approached me the wrong way*. Maybe they didn't know anything about my style or the direction of my company. I didn't feel like being their teacher. Maybe my customers wouldn't be remotely interested in their products, but the salesperson hadn't researched it. Some salespeople were too intimidated to give a proper presentation. Others were way too confident. Some folks acted like they were my best friends, but I never met them before.

A few salespeople were sent into battle *without any empowerment or knowledge*. They were the warrior foot soldiers and if they fell in battle, that was all right with their management. I could ask one million questions, but they didn't have many answers. I could make requests, but they would say, "let me get back to you after I talk to my boss." Their supervisor should have attended the meeting, but he chose to send in his salesperson. They were on a "search" mission and it didn't matter to them if they wasted my time, just as long as the salesperson came back with some information. In each of these cases, greater preparation and research might have improved their meeting with me.

Famous Objections

Let's assume that you are prepared for objections. Think of a few good objections you've heard during the course of your career:

We're not buying right now.
I'm overbought.
We're really very happy with the merchandise from our current supplier.
I don't understand what your product does.
How is your product different from what I carry and from what my competition buys?
It's not the right shape or color.
I hate the package.
It's too expensive.
I don't think we can sell it.
I just don't like it.
We only do category reviews once a year.

You've got to love the reasons and excuses that prevent a buyer from moving forward with your goods. I'm sure that most of what you're told is the truth, but you also must be aware that some buyers won't confront you with what they're *really* thinking. Are they looking at you in a funny way? Have you taken a shower recently?

You recall that there are all kinds of buyers out there, with different personalities and skill levels. Some buyers like to purchase everything; most are very selective about what they buy, and a few resist the temptation to ever spend any money. Be prepared for all that, and be ready for any question or comment that they throw your way.

This is a delicate balancing act. I've been in meetings with aggressive, heavily armed salespeople, feeling like I'm going mano a mano for 10 rounds in a steel cage match. On the one hand, you want to be prepared for all objections. However, if the meeting starts to become a "point/counterpoint" session, you could irritate the buyer.

Here's how this difficult situation is created. The buyer throws out an objection and you respond back with facts/benefits. That's good. It happens again 6 times, and you always have a comeback. If you have a buyer with an open mind, years of experience and the desire to improve their assortment, they will appreciate your approach. They want to buy. However, if the buyer is somewhat close minded and has too much ego involved, you could be involved in a tennis match, with each side lobbing the ball back over the net, in a never-ending war of wills.

Pay attention to your surroundings. If the buyer is fighting you, stop and regroup. What is going wrong with your strategy? Maybe you need to ask them. If the buyer is moving down the path towards a purchase, keep talking. My point here is that merely throwing out solutions and facts and benefits doesn't guarantee a sale.

If it's not clear why the buyer is resisting, go for the direct approach. What else can you provide to ease the buyer's worries? After all, isn't that part of the issue? Some buyers are afraid of making a mistake. If they get "hung" with inventory or a product that doesn't sell, doesn't that make them a pitiful buyer? Unfortunately, some folks believe that. I, however, opt for the opposing point of view, expressed by the old line: "no guts, no glory." If you don't take chances, you can never win. During the course of my career, I took innumerable chances. I'd listen to the salespeople only after I knew that they were trustworthy. They wouldn't want me to fail because their reputations were on the line as well. I had many "bad buys." Funny, but I can't remember any of them. I'm trying really hard to recall them, but I never kept any notes about them. A good buyer takes chances, monitors the success or failure of the sku, and takes quick action to liquidate any liability. My bad buys never hung around indefinitely—I always subscribed to the theory that the first markdown should be the deepest.

How can you take the fear out of this transaction? If their objection is the fear of failure, how can you ensure its success? Will you take the merchandise back if it doesn't sell? Are you offering demonstrators in some stores to help show this new product to the consumer?

You're a sales warrior. You've prepared for the buyer's meeting, you answered all their questions with detail, and you convinced them to buy. Make sure that the factory backs you up and ships the goods on time.

Now isn't that simple?

Chapter 8

How Does A Buyer Look At Things, Part 2 (<u>or are the buyers just insane?</u>): Advertising

In the Bible, Book of Ecclesiastes, Chapter 3, there is an extensive discussion on proper timing in life.

> To every thing there is a season, and a time to every purpose under the heaven.
> A time to be born, and a time to die; a time to plant, and a time to pluck up that which is planted;
> A time to kill, and a time to heal; a time to break down, and a time to build up;
> A time to weep, and a time to laugh; a time to mourn, and a time to dance;
> A time to cast away stones, and a time to gather stones together; a time to embrace, and a time to refrain from embracing;
> A time to get, and a time to lose; a time to keep, and a time to cast away;
> A time to rend, and a time to sew; a time to keep silence, and a time to speak;
> A time to love, and a time to hate; a time of war, and a time of peace.

Samurai Musashi talks about timing, too, but from a warrior's point of view.

THOUGHT #8

When you cross a sea, there are places called straits. Also, places where you cross a sea even twelve or fifteen miles wide are called fords. In going through the human world as well, there will be many points that could be called crossing a ford. On the sea lanes, knowing where the fords are, knowing the state of the boat, knowing the weather...you adapt to the state of the time, sometimes taking advantage of crosswinds...you take command of the ship and cross the ford. ...Sensing the state of opponents, aware of your own mastery, you cross the ford by means of the appropriate principles, just as a skilled captain goes over a sea-lane. ...To "cross a ford," put the adversary in a weak

62

position and get the jump yourself; then you will generally quickly prevail.[7]

Miyamoto Musashi

Musashi is discussing preparation, the impact of your environment, analyzing your competition and finding their weaknesses, being aware of your strengths, and waiting for the right moment to strike.

Buyers go through numerous considerations while they are strategizing their business. In this chapter, we will explore how buyers plan and time their advertising.

What thoughts stream through a buyer's mind when they're deciding what to advertise? Let me break down the process. Initially, buyers turn to the biggest unit and dollar movers in their assortment and plan them into ads. All retail stores have best selling items, and so do buyers. Out of the hundreds or thousands of skus under the care of a buyer, some may be in the store's top 100 bestseller list. Also, retailers regularly refer to the 80/20 rule—that 80% of sales are produced by 20% of the items. When a buyer chooses merchandise to advertise, they are guaranteed a strong response if best sellers—top 100 or 80/20 items—are promoted. Best sellers are in high demand and advertising them typically brings traffic into the store—more people looking to purchase these desirable goods, and that creates more rings in the cash register.

When a retail store is new, especially if it's a new concept, they try to sell consumers on buying from them. They are advertising the full store. Ads run in the formative days of Office Depot displayed the broad assortment of hardcore office products that we carried. We did show best sellers, but there were a whole lot of really weird and unusual products covered in the advertising as well. "We've got everything you need to run your business," was the unspoken statement made by the advertising.

As a retail store matures, each ad produces specific, and often large, sales results. At this point in the store's development, they are focused more on the selling of items as well as promoting the store. If a DVD player is on the cover of a circular and produces sales of $10 million for the week it is advertised, the buyer is up against that volume when they "anniversary" that ad one year later. This means that any ad running in the same spot in the following years weekly circular must generate sales exceeding the last benchmark of $10 million. If a weak item is placed on the cover, fewer customers will respond to the ad, the registers will not be ringing, and the overall store's sales will suffer. Retailers constantly compare their sales volume, looking at this years result vs. last years. The objective is to meet or exceed the planned percent increase. Advertising that doesn't drive the business above last year's levels is not considered successful.

With all the major retailers in America, and many smaller ones too, the concept of beating last year's ad results is well ingrained in the thought process. Ads will not be created if the buyer can't prove to their management that items recommended for promotional vehicles won't drive additional or incremental sales.

In most instances, the buyer is allocated a specific amount of space in the store's advertisements. Typical ad vehicles include: pages in the daily newspaper, multi-page circulars either inserted into the newspaper or direct mailed to the customer's home, postcards, letters, emails, television spots, or radio. A buyer may be given a small section of the store's ad to fill with their choice of goods, or to support a theme: back to school, holidays, all cleaning supplies, or a mobile office are examples. The retailer could have an eight page circular, but the buyer's ad space might be one box out of many in it, or maybe one item out of three products featured in a TV or radio spot. Some buyers have such large businesses that they run huge ads that offer only that buyer's merchandise. For example, the swimwear buyer might have a full-page newspaper ad at the beginning of the summer. Years ago, when I was buying for a department store in Georgia, I ran a four page newspaper insert with only telephone products. However, circulars run by stores typically have space doled out to many of their buyers, creating a larger product story across many pages.

If a buyer has lots of space to fill in an ad, they could offer top sellers as well as expose lesser-known items. Buyers handle numerous merchandise categories and, sometimes, they build advertisements displaying products from all their areas of responsibility. For example, when I was a housewares buyer, I'd regularly advertise large cookware stainless steel sets—two fry pans and three saucepans for a special price. They were my best sellers. However, I'd occasionally insert a small box into my ad space with a pressure cooker in it. I didn't sell many of those things, but I felt it was important to tell the consumer that my store had all types of cookware available for them to purchase. This maintained our image as a full-line store.

What size or space does a buyer need for their ad items? If it is a best selling item, producing huge dollars in sales, then the buyer is likely to consider a larger space. For example, a new, mega-processor laptop computer, with the latest technology that permits you to beam signals all the way to Pluto, needs a larger space to tell about its features and benefits, as well as provide a big photo for the consumers to review. That is an example of cutting edge technology that is promotional. However, if you have a basic item, like the biggest selling bag of dog food, you won't find that buried in an ad measuring one inch tall. Good sellers and interesting items will get moderate space. The "tonnage" items, on the other hand, usually get larger play in a retailer's ads.

Drama plays a role in advertising too. If the merchandise has a significant "offer" attached to it—50% off, or $5 off a $10 item—the customer is likely to get excited and come running in to buy it. The retail buyer is going to request more space and a prominent location in the store's advertising for such a great sales offer. Also, if the buying department believes that they can dramatize the presentation of the merchandise and sell more goods, they might go for a larger, more dramatic shot, even the full front cover.

If the marketplace has a retail price established on an item, and the buyer is able to provide a significant cost savings to the consumer, that warrants a large ad space with a dramatic layout. Let's suppose that a set of six, fine German knives—the type you'd find in the best kitchens in the world—sold regularly for $129.99. But through excellent negotiation with the supplier, a buyer gets a cost decrease and can run this product for $99.99, making the same margin dollars. That would be worthy of a larger space in an ad. It's a nice price savings over the regular retail and $99.99 has a better sound to it than $129.99. You can put the $99.99 in a really big font and show a $30 savings.

One retail store that employed me said this type of an ad was a **"drop the baby" offer**. Mom and dad are at home on a Sunday, reading the newspaper, rocking their baby to sleep in their arms. Suddenly, mom discovers the $99.99 knife offer, gets really excited, and in her haste to run to the store to get the deal, drops the baby. Well, the story goes something like that, but you get the idea. A dramatic offer sells a lot of merchandise.

High-low, Everyday Low, Regular, Original and List Prices

There are all kinds of retail pricing strategies designed to get consumers to respond to advertising. Many stores in America prefer to run sales events, and these retailers are called "high-low," meaning, their everyday prices are high, and they run goods on sale at a low price. Sale prices can be in effect for a few hours, one or two days, or for several weeks.

In the last ten to fifteen years, we've seen a proliferation of everyday low price retailers, and these stores carry the acronym EDLP. Warehouse style stores from clubs to office products chains to pet stores have utilized this method for selling their products. An EDLP store never runs sales; they are at an everyday low price all the time. When an EDLP retailer advertises, they are showing the consumer that they have low prices. High-low retailers, instead, are comparing their regular prices to lower sale prices.

Which format works better? You'd have to ask the consumer. I've worked for both types of stores and they both sell merchandise. When it comes to EDLP chains, shoppers love being able to get hot prices whenever they need to buy. However, customers also enjoy rushing into a store to get a hot bargain on sale. The problem with the high-low format is that it forces people to buy heavily on sale, but then purchases can trickle to lower numbers during non-sale times. A tremendous percentage of high-low retailer's volume occurs during sale events, making some of those stores ghost towns in non-ad periods. When I was a member of store management at department stores, you could roll a bowling ball down the aisles after a sale had ended and you wouldn't hit a customer. On the other hand, EDLP retailers tend to have more constant volume. If you'd graph high-low store's sales, they'd show a steep spike upwards during their ad events. EDLP stores have spikes when they run ads as well, but they also can have good sales even during times they're not running an ad.

High-low retailers often utilize words like "regular," "original" and "list" in their advertising copy. All three words compare high retails to current low sale prices. Here's how "regular" and "original" prices are established. Some stores bring limited inventory of an item onto their floors, setting a high retail for one to two months and then run it on sale. It's legal, but a clever way to manipulate the consumer. For example, let's suppose a buyer will be running sweaters on sale at Christmastime for $9.99. Prior to the holiday, they could land limited quantities of the clothes in select stores throughout their markets, and put them out in August at $19.99. By leaving the goods on the floor for a month or two at $19.99, they establish an "original" price. In October, they could drop their retail price to $14.99, bring in lots more inventory and advertise these goods—a 25% savings off the "original price." This reads like a sale to the consumer. In December, the buyer can run a sale on the sweaters at $9.99. Now, they're able to say either: 1) "Save 50% off original prices or; 2) $9.99, save $5 off regular price of $14.99. Both ways are legal and very attractive to the consumer.

Manufacturers typically set "list" prices as a *suggested* price. Normally, most stores ignore these suggestions. List prices were used extensively in the early years of the office supply chains, and I've seen them on sales floors of musical instrument chain stores too. You'd see an advertisement that said, "List price $100, sale $49.99. I've worked in more than six consumer product's industries, and I've found that list prices often were much higher than my most "extortionistic" retails.

To me, list prices and original prices are both *fictitious prices*. Retailers would be out of their minds to normally sell products at list or original prices—both are considerably higher than the actual selling prices you'd find in the marketplace. But the comparison of high list or original prices to the much lower sale prices creates a great value in the minds of the consumer. List and original prices are a legal device that high-low retailers employ to snare the consumer. Both methods are successful.

Here's the inside skinny on both list and original prices—they're typically way above the profit requirements of the retailer. Here's how they work. In the sweater scenario above, the actual cost might be $5. Let's suppose that the buyer's margin plan was 65%—a reasonably high profit number. When the product is at its original price of $19.99, the buyer's margin is 75%. At the regular price of $14.99, they're still making 66.6%, selling above the margin plan. Yet, $14.99 sounds like a good price to the consumer. When the retailer starts "closing out" the goods at the "bargain" price of $9.99, they're still earning a respectable 50%. Although it appears that prices are being slashed all along the way, in fact the store is making a pretty good profit at every turn.

There are various governmental groups that watch for truth in advertising. High-low retailers who run the same item on sale *every* month are viewed with jaundiced eyes. There must be off ad periods for this merchandise, otherwise it's really not a sale. Typically, one month without a lower price means that the goods have reverted back to their regular price. Then, you can run them on sale again.

So, what's a good ad? Is it a "drop the baby" type of offer? Does it incite the consumer to dash to their car and rush over to the store?

There is never a good sale for Neiman-Marcus unless it's a good buy for the customer.

Herbert Marcus
Co-founder, Neiman-Marcus

The best buyers in America look at their advertising this way—from the customer's point of view. What is the hot price in the marketplace? Can a lower price be offered without sacrificing profitability? How can the photography and copy for the ad scream VALUE to the consumer?

Prior to the ad ever running, the buyer has calculated the number of units likely to sell and what kind of "lift" is expected. The lift is the percent increase over regular sales. If a product normally sells 1,000 pieces a week without an ad, how much of an increase will occur by putting the goods on sale and notifying the consumer? A good ad has a healthy sales lift planned for the merchandise. The buyer considers how this product has sold in the past when placed on promotion, the impact of current business conditions and competitive activity, and the strength of the advertised offer.

The bottom line to advertising is *how did the ad perform*? Was the price competitive? Did the ad copy and photo properly display the product? Is the item desirable at any price? Was there enough inventory on the store shelves to support the demand? Should this item be jettisoned or advertised again under different conditions? The best retailers in America review the results of their advertising vs. the projected sales lift, and they learn how to improve their business in the future. If an ad didn't accomplish the projected sales, what was the reason? Was it a bad offer?

When to Advertise

If a great item is available from the supplier with a substantial offer, or savings, attached, the buyer then examines **when to advertise** and **where and how**. When to advertise depends on a variety of factors: has this merchandise been advertised recently or too frequently; does seasonality factor into the sales; what is the buyer's competition doing with these products; and does this merchandise fit into the theme of the advertising that the retail store is running during this time period?

Too much advertising is not a good thing for all merchandise. I once worked for a divisional merchandise manager who implored his buyers to take great sellers, plug them into numerous ads and "ride them like a race horse, whipping them for all they're worth, until the horse won't run anymore." Advertise the product until its sales die. Look in your newspaper and find the items that run every week. Yet this strategy also can wear out its welcome with the consumer—it makes for a boring, predictable ad. Also, there are retail laws at state level that prohibit keeping an item on sale for ridiculously long periods. The product must be off sale for a reasonable amount of time. So, if merchandise was recently advertised, the buyer might not put it back into a promotion right away.

If goods are seasonal, it might make sense to give them space in an ad. Likewise, if the season is ending, why would you want to advertise? Holiday-themed merchandise would be ridiculous if advertised in September. Flea medications for dogs rarely are shown during the winter (fleas are hibernating), but the summer months are perfect for a sale on these goods.

Any ad that the buyer runs must take into consideration what is happening in the marketplace. If the competition is blasting this product out at unearthly low prices, what does the buyer want to do about it? Depending on the management style of the retail corporation, I have been encouraged to ignore competition, to crush competition, or to match their prices in an ad. What manufacturer's merchandise is the competitor putting into their ads, how do they show the product graphically, and how does the competition's ad schedule on these products fit within their store's overall marketing plan?

If competition regularly runs items below cost, buyers have a choice whether to get into a price war on ad, look the other way, or find a way around this. Can the buyer advertise similar, but different products, to avoid a confrontation or is open warfare the only way to go? Often, suppliers will receive phone calls from distraught buyers, enraged that identical merchandise carried by their store and their competition is being offered at a lower price to the competition. How does the buyer know that absolutely? In truth, they don't, but they're seeing lower retail prices at their competition on the same merchandise, and are assuming that the supplier is giving better cost prices to them. If you are a manufacturer and put into a difficult situation because your products are being footballed around, should you confront the offending buyer and tell them to cease and desist? Nope—it's against the law, and we'll discuss that in a later chapter. But this is a common occurrence. Stand back and take a deep breath. Out with the bad air and in with the good air. Stores have the right to set crazy prices on your merchandise—but you can't tell them how to price the goods. The point here is that insane things do take place at retail, but the buyer must consider what their competition is doing before they put a sku on ad.

Can the buyer find merchandise that fits within an advertised storewide theme? There's "home for the holidays," with all merchandise that you might find in a house around holiday time: this could include bedding, furniture, electronics, housewares and food. "Dog days of summer," could be a beach theme, with iced beverage coolers, outdoor sun chairs, beach towels, hot dogs, sunscreen and more. You also see "white sales" for all bedding and bath items. Some stores have "founders day sales," or "anniversary sales," and spring, summer, fall and winter sales. These often feature goods across the entire spectrum of the store, looking to lure in huge groups of consumers. Around the Christmas timeframe, you see the proliferation of one- and two-day sales. Buyers are challenged to find the right merchandise to support these storewide events.

Where and How to Advertise

Above, we discussed when to run an ad. The buyer also faces the choice of **where and how to advertise**: should it be a national, regional or local ad and what vehicle should be utilized (circular, flyer, mailer, postcard, email, TV, radio or newspaper ad)?

The more sophisticated stores have to grapple with local market preferences, and their advertising reflects that. It is very common today for a buyer to have a TV ad that runs with one product in one location, but it is changed to different goods elsewhere. Your Sunday circulars are filled with the same thing. At the very least, prices vary by market today, and retailers can print ads for numerous price zones across the country. Often, they will offer different merchandise based on the needs of the local population. In sunny San Diego, there isn't a need to advertise raingear, and snow shovels would be totally ridiculous.

Weather is certainly a consideration. Also, demographics impact the advertising. For example, highly ethnic communities have special needs and products. If a retailer homogenizes their approach via advertising, they will not be attracting all the special customers in specific markets. Certain foods and drinks sell better in some parts of the country—you wouldn't want to run national ads on these. Retailers have been known to sell different wild birdseed in various regions, because you don't find the same birds everywhere. Buyers understand this and adjust their advertising accordingly.

Depending on the retail store, some buyers are given ad space and must fill it, with the choice of the best media picked by senior management. Every store has a preferred way to advertise. Mass-market stores and electronics chains have newspaper ad inserts every week on Sunday. They occasionally supplement that with TV commercials. It works for them. Another national retailer chooses monthly catalogs mailed to their customers, mixed with radio ads for sale periods. The advertising and marketing department for every store probably has tried a variety of media until they settled on ones that worked specifically for their products. However, a buyer often can recommend a strategy for their products that mixes several media together. At one company, their largest businesses required a mix of circulars, postcards, television and emails to get the products exposed. When I bought consumer electronics, my store gave me ad space in their circulars and newspaper ads. However, I devised a plan for dramatically growing the business and recommended a two-page spread (double truck) in the newspaper with *only* my merchandise. The management bought into my plan, and the ensuing ad grew my business by 35%. (I also had to anniversary that damned ad every year afterwards.) So buyers often have some latitude on what forms of media can be used for their ads.

Other Advertising Issues

There are a few other interesting things that a samurai salesperson needs to know about buyers and advertising, and I'm saving the juiciest tidbit for last. Please don't skip ahead. Pay attention!!

What about when the buyer is "hung" with an inventory problem? Should you advertise your way out of such a situation? Perhaps. It depends on the nature of the problem. If the merchandise is a good seller and doesn't have an issue with shelf life or an expiration date (like food), then a well-placed ad can move through some overstock. However, if the merchandise is starting to disintegrate, and is not increasing in value like fine wine, and the packaging is fraying, and mothers are fearful that their kids will contract a disease from going near the products, these are not the right items for an ad. You can't get the consumer to buy a "dog." If the product is howling on the shelf, find another way to liquidate it—but don't advertise. Work with your buyer on a solution.

Ads should not be put into production if there will be a potential supply problem. That's why the biggest and best stores heavily consult with their suppliers before booking an ad. This requires communication and a projected quantity buy, as well as a response that the manufacturer can deliver the full request and on time. Are you communicating with your buyer, inventory manager and factory about merchandise needs for upcoming ads? Do you know what the retailer is advertising in the future with you?

Strange things have happened to me during my career with ad goods. All buyers have been through **ad nightmares**. Vendors suddenly wake up to the fact that the units specified on the purchase order from the buyer don't agree with the quantities sitting in their warehouses. Ooops! Sorry. Wrong, you can't do that! If you accepted the purchase order from the retailer, they are expecting that you will ship goods to them. Some manufacturers have products that are so desirable, that they are playing "catch up" with the purchase orders. The factory is struggling to keep up with the demand. As a result, some vendors put goods on "allocation," a dirty word to all retail buyers. An allocation means that you will not get the full quantities ordered and that potential pandemonium will be created on the retail store sales floor. How can you help your buyers to avoid such problems? Can you give them concrete delivery dates for new merchandise? You must alert the buyer to all merchandise shortages and allocations. Ads with inventory problems can be avoided with stellar communication between you and your buyer.

Another retail nightmare has the buyer/assistant or buyer/inventory manager noticing that an ad scheduled to run in one week doesn't have any inventory to back it up at store level. Goods were ordered, but the vendor never called to mention a problem, and no merchandise has arrived. Most stores today have detailed systems and procedures in place to prevent this from happening. I often told the buyers reporting to me that ad inventory problems were unconscionable. It is the same as sending out invitations to a party at your house, but when your guests arrive, there's no food or drink available. It's rude and it enrages the consumer, who made a special trip to your store and can't find the merchandise. If you advertise it, you better

71

back it up with goods. Help the buyer by supporting this and ensuring that their ad goods have shipped on time.

To be fair, it's necessary to say that the vendor doesn't create all ad inventory problems. If a proper projection or purchase order isn't delivered on a timely basis, how can the manufacturer be expected to have enough inventory? In my experience, suppliers work extremely hard to anticipate the retailer's needs. I've known vendors who build complicated spreadsheets or utilize very sophisticated software to track a buyer's purchases, and build a forecast when the retailer didn't provide one. Oftentimes, basic, best selling items are in plentiful supply at most factories. However, there are occasions when better communication between the buyer and seller could improve ad inventory flow. If you're a samurai salesperson, you won't let your company get into a difficult situation. Instead, ask for the purchase orders and projections; and regularly discuss advertising and when the ads are running. As you've gathered, the buyer's life is hectic, so it's ok for you to ask them about upcoming ads and the inventory needs.

Are You Spending Ad Dollars Wisely?

All right. You've been very patient. Let's talk about some of the favorite advertising questions for salespeople calling on retail buyers. "We give the buyer all this ad money and they don't run enough ads to spend it, but they collect the money anyhow." Or, I've been asked, "with all the ad coop dollars a buyer gets from us, am I really spending my company's (manufacturer's) money wisely?"

Many retailers believe that if you've agreed to a total year's financial program—with coop advertising funds, rebates, quick-pay dating and more—and sales objectives are hit, you should be happy and give the buyer all the funds. The big stores may not be able to run an ad that spends your coop dollars by showing your products, but those retailers feel that your funds are put towards advertising the store via TV or other ways you wouldn't notice. If the advertising pulls in customers, and your products are being purchased, why aren't you happy? If you're satisfied with your sales volume at a retailer, I recommend that you pay them the agreed upon incentives.

However, if the question you're asking is, "am I really spending my company's money wisely," you need to judge that yourself. The bigger question is if you should invest your money in other ways with the retailer. You do need to investigate this point. We'll fully cover all incentive programs in a later chapter, but let me give you a glimpse now. You need to find out which incentives are important to your customer, the buyer.

Although most of the retailers that I've known had a critical need for ad funds, I've also worked for one giant retailer that had an internal budget for advertising. That corporation was more concerned that buyers extract a big rebate from vendors. My annual review and bonus was dependant on rebate dollars, but *not* coop advertising. Ask other vendors who do business with your buyer and question the buyer as well. "If I gave you these funds as a rebate, quick pay discount or something else, would that be more meaningful to you?" Here's the real question: "Does a buyer get credit for coop ad allowances?" If the answer is 'yes,' keep the ad monies coming and try to help the buyer to develop a dynamic plan for the fiscal year. If the buyer doesn't benefit from coop allowances, and you're not happy with your sales results, you need to have a discussion and plan another way to spend your incentive funds.

Chapter 9

How Does A Buyer Look At Things, Part 3: Vendors

In the movie, "The Wizard of Oz," Glinda the good witch of the North asks Dorothy, "Are you a Good Witch or a Bad Witch?" Dorothy replies, "Who me? Why, I'm not a witch at all." (Metro-Goldwyn-Mayer, 1939).

Retail buyers are basically asking the same question. Are you a good vendor or a bad vendor? Can they depend on you for all their needs? Will your performance be exemplary or confounding?

When a buyer chooses to do business with you, do you understand the decision-making that has taken place? Why did they choose you and agree to do business? Is it because you have products that they critically need? Probably. There are many concrete reasons why a buyer would purchase your goods.

Buyers would prefer to transact business with good vendors. If people naturally gravitate towards pleasure and away from pain, and if low maintenance vendors should be rewarded with expanded business, doesn't it behoove you to be a good vendor?

Here's how I always defined a "good vendor." There are essentially five components:

1. **Quality products**
2. **On time delivery & quality service**
3. **Competitive prices**
4. **Great communication**
5. **Cutting edge goods and new items**

Each of the above factors is critical to your business. If a trade partner adopted four out of five parts, the likelihood for future success is diminished. You really need to master all five items. Let me explain.

Quality products are a top priority. I know, there are folks reading this who are laughing because this should be obvious, but not every factory creates quality merchandise. Not every store in the USA requires quality. But for the majority of retailers out there, quality is the number one most important feature; they don't want to disappoint the consumer and have goods returned because they break or don't live up to expectations.

If you sell quality products and deliver them to the retailer exactly *when* their purchase orders request, you're winning most of the battle. Many salespeople believe that **on time delivery** has a certain amount of latitude built into it, that hitting the purchase order delivery date is open to some interpretation. It isn't. You need to fully understand if "receive date" or "delivery date" means dropping the goods at the retailer's store or warehouse before the date, exactly on that day, or within a window of days afterwards. In my experience, the delivery date was very specific, and if you missed it and delivered late, by days or weeks, you were bringing hardship to the retailer.

Here's why an imprecise delivery date hurts a retailer. Inventory managers and buyers for retail stores have cut down on the amount of goods sitting on the shelves and in the warehouses to low levels to optimize their turn. If you run into a problem and don't deliver on the specified date, goods are continuing to sell at store level, and the purchase order wasn't built to account for this. Should one week go by before your goods arrive, the purchase order really should have been increased by one-weeks worth of goods. Buyers will tell you about their experiences of having products arriving one month or later. Remember, buyers prefer low maintenance vendors. If you can't deliver on time and your product is a commodity, they might eventually start giving your business to your competitor. Quality products are useless if they are delivered late.

On time delivery is part of **quality service**. Let me give you an example of a wonderful supplier with great service. This vendor had annual cost sales of $5 million, with my business contributing approximately 30% of his total. He was one of my smaller volume suppliers, but he offered products that were unique in the marketplace. One day, I ran into a problem with his merchandise—it was a food item needing special handling. However, my store's warehouse was short staffed, forcing them to ship goods without a full inspection. My vendor's warehouse was heavily guarded for bugs and treated regularly for infestation. Yet, coming into Christmas, the shipment received at my stores was loaded with creepy crawlers. It didn't matter to me where the bugs entered the distribution pipeline, although my warehouse probably was at fault. I wanted the problem to go away quickly. When notified, the vendor volunteered to take the goods back and rapidly replaced them with new merchandise. He had to destroy the infested goods. It cost him a bundle to take this action and dramatically impacted his financials for that year, but he felt compelled to help me. We averted a holiday disaster as a result, and I never forgot how he supported my store. As a result, I offered him every opportunity to grow his business in the future, often taking over categories from weaker vendors.

Quality products delivered on time also need to be **competitively priced**. This doesn't mean that you have to be the lowest price, just competitive. Certainly, there are buyers who shop for the lowest price available, but more experienced, "seasoned professional buyers" understand that price isn't the only determining factor. Assuming that you sell to a store that offers moderate to better quality merchandise, you need to be competitively priced. Samurai salespeople pay attention to their competition and study how retailers are pricing competitive merchandise. If you understand the margin requirements retailers have, and notice that a competing product seems to be selling for an unusually low price, has the competiting factory cut the invoice cost? Don't let your competition embarrass you. Do retailers tell you that your merchandise is too expensive or that others, offering comparable goods, provide better prices? Are you ignoring their comments or investigating them?

Let's suppose that your quality goods are delivered on time, but your company's internal profit structure requires a very high price in comparison to your competition. You may find some retailers who will buy from you, but most will eventually ignore your products. It does catch up to you.

Now, you may ask, "Mr. Samurai Merchant, why are you putting **communication** on this list?" Because if you manufacture quality products, deliver them on time, are competitively priced, but can't communicate with buyers, you will fail. How is it possible that everything can be going right, but communication will bring you down?

Here are a few of my experiences with poor communicating salespeople. A buyer explains to a manufacturer that other vendors are attempting to steal their business, and the salesperson doesn't tell his headquarters. Eventually, the competition takes over all the business. Or, a buyer is feeling mistreated, perceiving that a vendor is giving superior service to the buyer's competition. But the salesperson doesn't fully understand these comments, passes them on to their superiors in a garbled form and nothing happens (but the buyer does resent the inactivity). Similarly, pieces of business are siphoned off in another direction.

Big suppliers can fall into another trap. They're delivering name brand goods, on time, at a competitive price, but they don't have a desire to listen to the buyer's special needs—things requested by the buyer's corporation. The buyer's management might want new packaging, special signing, increased financial incentives or a multitude of other things. However, the manufacturer doesn't feel like supporting any of these concepts. Instead of explaining their point of view, the salesperson stonewalls or ignores the buyer's requests. This is embarrassing for the buyer, making it appear that they're ineffective. I once heard a merchandise manager tell a buyer in this situation, "so, could you please tell me the name of the buyer that is managing this vendor?" Bad communication styles stymie the buyer's efforts and give the impression that the buyer isn't much of a negotiator—nothing is getting accomplished. The buyer is forced to do business with these vendors, but hates it, and if they can move some of their business to a vendor who does communicate and support them better, they will.

Lastly, a good vendor will offer **cutting edge** and **new products** on a regular basis. When I was in the office products business, I recall the top branded supplier proudly stated, "We take 25% of our profits and plow them back into research and development of new products." In another industry, a manufacturer proclaimed, "At any given time, over 10% of our skus are new products."

What type of image do the statements above create? Factories that are leading a category, paving the way and are the industry's experts make those assertions. If you are a consumer shopping for the best product to solve a problem or need, won't you gravitate towards an industry leader's merchandise? Buyers are committed to staying ahead of their competition and one way is to consistently purchase goods from the leading factory. Differentiation is key to attracting customers. If a buyer's store is different or superior because they purchase from the leading edge manufacturers with the newest merchandise, doesn't that make the shopping experience stronger?

Cutting Edge Manufacturers

Every industry has manufacturers who are renown for their dedication to the creation of cutting edge products. In electronics, Phillips and Sony co-designed the compact disc. In office products, 3M (Minnesota Mining and Manufacturing) developed Post-it notes and many other items. The Avery Dennison Corporation has a slew of amazing products—paper goods to design business cards, greeting cards, high gloss brochures and many more, at home, on your computer. In musical instruments, why are names like Fender and Yamaha cited as tops in their field? Every consumer products industry has manufacturers that push the envelope, have a desire to improve their goods beyond today's standards, and to be known for their ingenuity. Microsoft has been exceptionally aggressive in the marketplace, and they can be applauded for changing an industry via their ongoing innovations.

Does a supplier have to be "cutting edge" to consistently score points with retail buyers? It helps. There are perfectly successful manufacturers who sell quality products that are competitively priced, ship them on time, and communicate well with the buying team. But what happens when another vendor comes along who has the latest and greatest product? If there is a war going on at retail, and every buyer wants to set their store apart from the competition, cutting edge product gives sizzle to an assortment. Cutting edge products attract the consumer. If a retailer offers toothpaste and a leading supplier develops a product for quickly whitening teeth, that store immediately needs to purchase that great new item. What would happen to that store if it didn't offer it for sale? Clearly, making the correct decision can affect a retailer's market share.

IAMS dog and cat foods are perceived by the consumer to be a leading edge product. Prior to the year 2000, if you wanted to buy IAMS foods, you'd have to visit a pet specialty store. Soon after Procter & Gamble acquired IAMS in 1999, they made a considerable strategy change. In 2000, IAMS chose to dramatically expand their distribution, selling their products to grocery, warehouse club and mass-market stores. What ensued was a stampede heading to those retailers. Stores in America had to carry this brand or be perceived in a negative light. Carrying the IAMS line immediately gave the grocery/warehouse club/mass market stores the image of being cutting edge.

Five Critical Components

What if one of the five components above was removed? If goods were top quality, cutting edge and priced fairly, but the manufacturer couldn't deliver on time, how long would a buyer want to continue doing business with them? Now, in this situation, because the products might be revolutionary, the buyer might cut the vendor some slack due to start up problems. But if every time they rolled out new goods the same issues arose—inability to deliver at the promised time—the buyer would start to question the relationship. What if the retailer had inserted this great new product into an advertisement and then failed to hit a target date? Ouch!!

As you can see, each of the five components above is important to your success. There are cases that defy this logic, however. If you manufacture quality, cutting edge products, deliver on time and have great communication with your customers, you may not have to be totally competitively priced. Revolutionary, state of the art, brand-spankin'-new products are somewhat removed from this rule. The first CD player was not priced at $99.99—they couldn't and they didn't need to do that. Leading edge product normally can command any price the marketplace will bear. Then, as competition jumps on the bandwagon and creates their version of the hot product, prices start to drop and become competitive.

Let's not forget a critical 6th component necessary to be a good vendor: **profitability**. If the retail store can't make a decent profit on your merchandise, will they continue to purchase it? Of course, there are examples of commodity items that lose money, break even or barely earn a profit. Some unfortunate retail chain store buyers must stock these goods. I've been in other situations where commodities weren't involved and it was extremely difficult to make money on an item. Naturally, even though it wasn't the vendor's fault, the supplier was blamed for the insanity of my competition. I can recall very nasty times when I was competing with Macys, Sam's Club and Wal-Mart, among others. The vendor was accused of giving a better deal to those stores and often was encouraged to help me cover my margin losses. At times like these, smart, aggressive vendors find ways to help the retailer, because the buyers are beside themselves with anguish.

Merchandise profitability can tie directly to a manufacturer's distribution policy. For example, if a vendor chooses to sell multiple channels of distribution—department, specialty and mass market stores simultaneously—invariably, someone in that mix is going to crush the retail price. Some manufacturers intentionally sell *only* to a specific channel, like department stores, to keep prices elevated and the image of the item pristine.

Once a vendor crosses the line, and offers their goods to many different types of stores, the gloves are off and you are bound to see wacky retail prices in the market. The manufacturer can control whom they sell to and should do so with care and reflection.

When products cease to be profitable and a vendor's policies are hurting a retailer, the buyer has no choice but to look for other options. For example, when I was told, "I don't control the retails in the marketplace—it's against the law," I reacted accordingly to that lack of sympathy. If an item were available from a multitude of sources in a similar style, I'd buy it from someone else. Keep the buyer's merchandise profitable and you'll sleep better at night.

THOUGHT #9

A good vendor handles details and eliminates problems because the buyer is too busy.

We're talking about great service as a mandatory part of doing business with the buyer. Is your fill rate outstanding? Are you meeting your fill rate commitments? If a purchase order has 12 skus with 1,000 pieces required for each, are you shipping every single piece? What did you commit to the retailer? If you are regularly missing your obligations, are you reimbursing the retailer for lost sales? Yes, if you don't ship merchandise, the retailer can't sell it. I've often told suppliers that putting a photograph of the product on an empty shelf won't satisfy the consumer. "Well," you could tell the customer, "this is what the merchandise looks like." A retailer is out of business without merchandise. Are you helping the buyer with their commitment to the customer?

Retailers call their best selling goods "key items," or "top sellers" or "80/20 items." You have to especially protect these skus. If customers walking into a store can't find them, they will immediately head to another retailer. Keep supply problems away from your buyer by solving them before they occur. If you do have an issue, talk with the retailer's inventory specialists or buyers and try to fix things quickly. Let the buyer know how hard you are working on the problem, what is wrong, when you think you can resolve it and apologize for the inconvenience. But you must communicate with your buyer and not allow a stock issue to drag on indefinitely.

Good vendors also talk to the sales associates in a buyer's stores to find if they like or need the products. Are there any product issues that the sales associate is aware of? Are there any customer comments? Do you truly understand your customer (the buyer) and your customer's customer (the sales associate and the end user)? The buyer is thinking, "Has the vendor totally researched my store and my competition?" Good vendors consider all these questions and take action.

A good vendor gets involved with other things as well. If you are dealing with a headquarters location, does the manufacturer have a local, dedicated salesperson calling on the retailer and providing rapid responses to all questions? Good vendors have programs in place for not only handling customer returns but damages as well.

Critical financial packages are a significant part of doing business with retailers today. Do you have an effective coop and rebate deal with your buyer? Does it provide an incentive for the retailer to drive more business in your direction? A good vendor regularly reviews the success of their financial programs and adjusts them when necessary. We'll have a full discussion on financial incentives in a later chapter.

Buyers also will tell you, tongue in cheek, that a good vendor never gives them a price increase and offers special "net" terms—net never. Payment terms normally could include "N30" or net 30, meaning the full net invoice is due and payable within 30 days. "Net never" extends such payment terms into the next millennium. Good vendors understand this is a joke.

Chapter 10

Inventory Management

Buyers choose a vendor and their products and want the goods to flow smoothly, without headaches or interruptions. If you provide that, you are a good vendor.

Inventory management is part of a retailer and vendor's job. When goods are shipping on time to the stores, everyone is happy. Part of your knowledge base as a samurai salesperson needs to include an understanding of the flow and budgeting of inventory. Good vendors comprehend the retail adherence to "open to buy."

Open to buy is a budget that buyers and inventory folks utilize. Typically, department store buyers work with open to buy, and other major corporations stick to similar methods for controlling their budgets. If a buyer has "open to buy," that's good for you, their vendor—it means they have money budgeted and open to spend on more inventory. They have cash to buy your products.

Here's the formula for open to buy when inventories are tracked at cost:

The starting point is the inventory position at the beginning of a given month.

Take beginning of month (BOM) opening inventory (at cost) and then subtract:

- Sales (at cost)
- Returns to vendor (damages or authorized returns)

Then add to that number:

+ Merchandise Received
= Ending Inventory

Then, take the beginning of the next month's inventory plan and subtract the ending inventory from the previous month.

= Open To Buy.

Example:
June's BOM inventory = $100 (at cost)
- $20 Sales (at cost)

81

- $5 Returns to vendor (at cost)
= $75
+ $15 Merchandise Received (at cost)
= $90 ending inventory

If next month's (July) beginning of month (BOM) inventory plan is $100, the buyer will have $10 open to buy to spend on new merchandise.

July BOM inventory plan = $100

$90 ending inventory in June
= $10 open to buy

The buyer is able to purchase $10 in this scenario, which would bring their inventory levels back up to the July plan.

Open to buy budgeting is fluid and changes based on actual results. For example, if the buyer's department (above) missed sales plan and only sold $10, and then the ending inventory would have risen by $10 to $100. In this case, the buyer would have hit the inventory budget and would be unable to buy more goods.

Buyers adhering to the open to buy approach must also cut purchases if sales are declining. For example, if the buyer had placed purchase orders for future months that were based on a strong sales trend continuing, they would need to cut some of these orders to hit their inventory plans if business became soft.

Why do you need to know this? All buyers and inventory people have some sort of budget. If business is thriving, they're increasing orders and expecting you to drive the factory as hard as you can to deliver more, more, more. If conditions change, and the consumers are staying at home, they will need to cut back future purchases. A samurai salesperson stays watchful for any trends and adjusts their business accordingly. If the buyer is telling you that business is hurting, but they have many purchase orders placed with you for later months, you need to face the fact that they might cut back their business with you down the road.

Buyers and inventory managers have other considerations. When they're planning to run merchandise in an ad, they're considering how much inventory will be needed. If an item was advertised previously, there's some historical information that needs to be reviewed. If it wasn't advertised before, are there similar items that were advertised? How well did those items sell? How many pieces did they sell? What kind of sales increase or lift was achieved during the last promotion? How many pieces should be left on the shelf after the ad has run? How much lead-time is required for the vendor to deliver the goods on time? In short, there are ways to calculate how this merchandise will sell and how much is needed to buy.

Inventory Turn

The inventory managers and buyers also are critically examining how the merchandise you sold them is turning. Do you remember how to calculate inventory turn?

Annual Sales at cost/Average inventory = T/O (turn over)

How do you define inventory turn over, and why is it important to the retailer?

Inventory turnover equals the number of times their inventory sells out in one year.

You must understand that a retailer has several large investments—people and salaries, real estate, and inventory—and they must get a proper return on those investments. Depending on the item and product category, goods can be fast turning or slow. With the exception of best sellers, bookstores and compact disc stores have slow turning inventory. Consider the vast number of titles those stores carry and the few items that the public will passionately buy. That contributes to slow turn. However, without the broad assortment of products at those stores, customers wouldn't enjoy shopping them. You can't "browse" in a bookstore with only the top 25 best sellers.

The retail buyer and inventory manager are keeping their eyes on the merchandise turn and making adjustments when needed. The profit of the corporation can be thrown out the window if poor inventory decisions are made. It's a very precise operation. Keep the shelves looking full, but not too full. Keep minimal inventory in the warehouses because goods there aren't immediately available for sale. Keep the merchandise flowing from the vendors, set to arrive exactly at the perfect time. Keep the stuff turning. The more times the goods turn, the better return the store gets on their inventory dollars.

I've seen retail stores go through cyclical stages with their inventory. Very peculiar attitudes are visible during this time period. I call it a "pendulum effect." The pendulum swings to the far left and the retail management is screaming for more sales. Damn the inventory, full speed ahead. Business conditions may have deteriorated and the store needs volume quickly. They run sales and buy inventory in quantity to get a discount from the vendor. Retail prices are lowered to make the store more attractive to the consumer.

Then, they wake up from their drunken stupor and attitudes start to change. The inventory is piled to the sky and profitability is eroding due to lowered retail prices. The vendors didn't totally give away the farm. Senior management is freaking out. The pendulum has swung far to the right. "Quick, you idiots, get the inventory in line and look at your margins. Why are you giving these products away below your margin plan?"

When the inventory turn goes to hell, inventory managers and buyers are cutting back on their open purchase orders and bashing their vendor's brains in. Deal-making isn't performed with surgical precision but with a ball-peen hammer; hence the phrase "hammering out an agreement." It's a poignant time, especially if you're the supplier getting hammered. I've seen goods shipped back to suppliers in truckloads, or "rammed down their throats," as the case might be. Advertising is increased to help excite the consumer and to drive sales, and the unsuspecting/unprepared vendors are sent the bill.

Yes, when the pendulum is swinging, the buying office is churning and you'd best get out of the way.

Chapter 11

Know Your Merchandise and Uphold Professionalism

THOUGHT #10

...Observe the personal character of adversaries, find out people's strengths and weaknesses, maneuver in ways contrary to opponent's expectations, determine opponent's highs and lows, ascertain the rhythms in between, and make the first move; this is essential. If your own power of insight is strong, the state of affairs of everything will be visible to you. ...You will be able to figure out the minds of opponents and thus find many ways to win. This demands work.[8]

Miyamoto Musashi

Why are some people considered experts? Haven't they immersed themselves in every detail pertinent to a topic? We listen to experts on television and read their observations in the daily newspaper. Should we invest in a particular stock, or will a political gamble pay off—experts have formulated a point of view and are broadcasting their brilliance to the rank and file of America. How will a battle play out and how can the opposing army devise a strategy to win. Experts are considering the ways.

You must be an expert on your adversary—your competition—your products, the company you represent and your customer. The retail buyer will expect nothing less from your performance. You must be an expert about the history of your customer, how the retailer goes to market, what kind of products they like to carry, the personality of their store, their margin structure, their competition—everything about the retailer. In addition, you must possess intimate details about your company and the products they manufacture. You have to know everything about your merchandise, or you shouldn't be allowed out of your office.

Why am I hammering this point? There are salespeople on this planet who slough off product presentations with minimal thought or enthusiasm. These are folks who give salespeople a bad name. The retail samurai salesperson wouldn't get caught in this trap. I remember meeting with a peddler one day, and he was carrying a 5-inch ring binder filled with over thirty index tabs. He represented thirty different manufacturers and was making a half-hearted attempt to sell me on the qualities of at least ten of them. He'd flip to a tab, open a section, briefly discuss the manufacturer on that page and their goods, and move to the next tab. The presentation wasn't focused and it rambled during the hour-long session. Finally, running out of gas—or maybe it was my snoring that broke his reverie—he tried to quickly sell me on the merits of the tenth product line. He was rushing through the merchandise, going through the motions, failing to capture my interest, but I was convinced that he would tell the tenth factory that he had made a presentation about their line to the buyer of a well-respected store.

I have experienced this many times over my 25-year career and have heard similar tales from other buyers. If we agree that the buyers today don't have an abundance of time, why would you toss off a presentation and impress the buyer with your mediocrity? It's unprofessional, accomplishes nothing, wastes time and will insure that the buyer doesn't return your phone calls in the future. Be detailed, stay focused, and show your expertise.

Chapter 12

How Does A Buyer Look At Things, Part 4:

Space on the Sales Floor, Markdowns, Rebates and Incentives, Packaging, Imports (and other weird stuff)

THOUGHT #11

"To become the enemy" means to think yourself into the enemy's position.... In large-scale strategy, people are always under the impression that the enemy is strong, and so tend to become cautious.... In single combat also you must put yourself in the enemy's position. If you think, "Here is a master of the Way, who knows the principles of strategy," then you will surely lose. You must consider this deeply.[9]

Miyamoto Musashi

Mushashi had a way with words. What a clever way of saying that know-it-alls cannot succeed. You must delve into the thought process of your customer and your competition. But when the day comes that you think you have "mastered" their thinking, you may be setting yourself up for failure.

The wise retail samurai salesperson knows a great deal, but is open minded and constantly learning about new things all the time. Let's dig into some topics that should be familiar to you and examine them deeply. In this chapter, we'll investigate how buyers allocate space on the selling floor; markdowns, rebates and incentives; how the product is selling; packaging (the silent salesperson); and imports.

Space on the Sales Floor

Depending on the retail organization, a buyer can have absolute authority and control of the layout of their merchandise on the selling floor, or they are limited to only offering suggestions to store operations. Typically, the store's personnel appreciate the buyer's input and they attempt to design or lay out the sales floor to reflect the buyer's vision. A buyer might suggest that merchandise is stacked in their cartons on the selling floor with a sample taken out of the box and placed on top. But the actual execution might be lacking. I've found hot products still on the shelves in the back storage room, or buried under tables on the sales floor, invisible to the consumer. It makes you want to cry—or rant and rave.

Buyers across America will tell you about their frustrations trying to enact a "look" on the sales floor. You often can tell how long someone has been a buyer by his or her attitude towards product presentation at store level. Young buyers are hopeful and fight forcefully to recreate merchandise displays in a precise fashion. Older buyers accept the inevitable—they're lucky to see anything that vaguely resembles their ideas on the sales floor and won't get upset. One samurai retail manager I knew believed in the "law of thirds." He was convinced that one-third of all store personnel would successfully execute a concept, the next one-third would detail it correctly when they "got the chance," and the final third was comprised of losers and miscreants who'd never complete the project. I've found that the "law of thirds" has application to many things in life as well.

Assuming that the buyer does have some control of their merchandise in the store, how are goods displayed? Most merchandise can be found in one of two places: a home location or an off-shelf presentation. A home location is an area dedicated to similar products from a category. For example, you could find all music boom boxes grouped together on the back wall of a store. That is their home location. If one boom box was at a hot promotional price, or on ad (being advertised), it could be stacked out on the selling floor near the boom box wall or piled up in another part of the store. That is an off-shelf presentation. Off-shelf means that the merchandise is featured away from its assigned section to draw extra attention to an item.

The trim-a-tree Christmas department often has a home territory carved out in department stores. Also, stores will expand the presentation by putting Christmas merchandise on holiday themed tables, or outposts, in other parts of their store. These off-shelf presentations spread out the impact of the products. If you're a consumer who never ventures into that part of the store, they make you aware that the goods are available.

Planograms

In some stores, products are assigned specific locations on the sales floor, on fixtures, or on walls, with their placement precisely detailed on paper. That is called a planogram, which is a road map telling the store's personnel exactly where to put the merchandise. The layout or positioning of a product within a planogram is a reflection of buying patterns and aesthetics. If the shopping patterns indicate that merchandise placed at eye level will sell in greater quantities, the buyer will create a planogram with their best sellers in the key locations.

A planogram on a fixture will reflect the buyer's artistry as well—how can you make the merchandise more appealing to the consumer? The perfect arrangement on a shelf or fixture will attract the customer to the merchandise; an ineffective, dull layout of goods will cause the folks to walk on by. For example, when I was in the office supply business, I had 6 different "flavors" of colored file folders: blue, green, red, yellow, gray, and orange. Each shelf in the file folder section of the store had room for 6 boxes across. I'd take one box of each color (a total of 6 different colored boxes) and planogram it on the shelf. By duplicating that arrangement on the two shelves below it, you'd get a vertical striped row of blue, then green, then red and so on. Striping by color can create an eye-catching design.

Although planogram software can totally arrange the placement of merchandise, most stores do incorporate the human element to insure that the section looks appealing to the eye. This means many retailers physically set merchandise on fixtures to see how they look before they create the final planogram. There are no guarantees to the process. Depending on the buyer' skill level, they either can develop a planogrammed section that pops and draws your attention, or something that captures your eye because it seems like products were thrown against a wall. A men's room after a rock concert might look more appealing if the buyer is devoid of talent when it comes to product presentation.

Then there's the horizontal vs. vertical schools of thought. Some folks like arranging products clear across a shelf, spreading the next category on the shelf below. Other people believe that merchandise is more appealing to the eye when it's striped vertically. It's a matter of good taste vs. bad taste. I, for example, have excellent taste. I prefer vertical striping.

Be aware that some retailers have a different attitude towards merchandise presentation and don't utilize planograms. This is a more artistic approach. Fashion merchants devise all kinds of clever displays with clothing and change them frequently on the sales floor to keep the store's appearance constantly in a state of evolution. It keeps shoppers on their toes—you never know what to expect when you enter their stores. The motivation is to keep the store looking fresh.

Some other retail stores don't use planograms or artistic presentation methods. I'd call their approach, "who did it and ran?" Usually, the creator of this monstrosity isn't hanging around to show you the intricacies of their concept (because they didn't have one). These design wizards don't understand the relationship between attractive merchandising and increased sales. This school of thought values speed over beauty and expects the consumer to work before they buy any goods. Why make the customer's lives easier? Finding merchandise quickly? Hell, let them forage through the stack of goods. I'm sure that you've seen this approach in a few stores. Makes you want to linger in the store, right?

Where to Put Promotional Merchandise

Most stores have a system for presenting their merchandise in an attractive, appealing way. After the home locations are filled as described above, buyers set out to pick items for displays and promotional space. These special areas in the store focus on merchandise that is new, sharply priced, advertised or unique in some way. Promotional goods are placed on: pallets, endcaps, wings, power panels, clipstrips, cash register aisles, tables, bins, corrugated fixtures, and even can be stacked outside the store.

Pallets are made out of wood, typically used for shipping large items, raising the goods a few inches off the ground. You can find pallets on sales floors with all kinds of products stacked on top of them: boxed items, food in large bags and other things. You'd find pallet displays in warehouse clubs, grocery, and some other specialty stores with sufficient floor space. Filling a pallet requires a large inventory investment.

Endcaps are huge product presentations at the end of an aisle, often seen in grocery stores—think of canned items in the shape of a wall. These displays place goods in a pile stacked from floor to ceiling. The intent is to capture your attention with quantity of merchandise and a hot selling price. You also can find endcaps on floor gondola fixtures. Typically, endcaps require a substantial investment in extra inventory.

In the early days of the office supply superstores, merchandise filled their endcaps, many rows deep and heaped ten feet high. It was a macho presentation, with no regard for inventory turn. The message was a bold one, telling customers that these stores were in a heavy stock position and could quickly fill the business customer's needs. We were buying in truckload quantities, getting great price discounts and passing them on to the consumer. I remember when those towers of goods were analyzed and everyone changed their attitude—the endcaps were killing the turn. We didn't dismantle the endcaps, but we did find some very creative ways of lowering the number of units on display.

Tiny products don't deserve endcap space because the number of units to fill it would be prohibitive. However, if it's a larger product it can work well in this space. You can see endcaps made of canned foods, moderate sized boxed goods, luggage, cookware, pet food bags, and many other things.

Wings and *power panels* often are strapped to the sides of endcaps, at the ends of aisles. Warehouse styled stores can stack small quantities of goods on either side of an endcap, fanning out like a wing. A power panel is a little board filled with a few items that are smaller in size. In both of these cases, there is limited inventory investment, but the sales impact of this space can be significant, nevertheless.

I'm sure that you've all seen *clipstrips* hanging throughout many retail establishments. This promotional device ties small items onto a plastic strip, or something like it, and hangs off of metal shelving. When all the goods have been removed from the strip, it is thrown away and another clipstrip can replace it. I've seen great clipstrips of lip balm, razor blades, squeaky pet toys, and potato chips. There's less of an inventory investment here, and the retail prices are usually very low. You normally wouldn't find a $50 item hanging on a clipstrip. However, merchandise selling for under $10 can be effective.

Grocery stores are notorious for their successful placement of products in the *check out* and *cash register lanes*. Gum, candy, magazines, batteries, and other highly impulse-purchased goods have been found in this location. Other items can fit here as well, but they must be low priced, easily identifiable and with a high demand.

How do buyers pick items for displays and promotional space? It depends on a variety of factors. Basic merchandise that sells in huge quantities, day after day, is perfect for special promotional space. Consumers react strongly to some goods when they're put on sale at dramatic low price—these deserve promotional space. If the manufacturer is closing out a product, and the retailer buys quantity at a great savings, put that "bad boy" out in a promo area. Also, new, revolutionary merchandise is exciting to the customer and should be featured in a highly visible spot.

The buyer evaluates the merits of their products and chooses carefully before suggesting its placement in a promotional location. Large items will fit on an endcap or pallet drop. Medium sized goods can work on an endcap, pallet drop or wing. Smaller goods can fit on a wing, power panel, clipstrip, or be placed near the cash registers.

How can you, the samurai salesperson, make a suggestion to the buyer so that your merchandise qualifies for promotional space? Be certain that the products meet the criteria described above. If it's a "nice item," that doesn't mean that it deserves to get an extra display on the selling floor. Remember the chapter covering GMROI? The inventory folks and buyers have to evaluate if the extra sales and increased inventory will throw off a proper return on the investment. Think like a merchant and work on the numbers. If it adds up, suggest the product to the buyer for promotional space.

Signing is requisite for promo space. A pile of goods without a sign will qualify you to be a member of the "who did it and ran" club. Most customers don't have psychic powers (except in many parts of California). Don't expect them to intuitively understand that stacked out merchandise means "on sale." Then, what is the price? We've invited the customer into our store and they have limited time to spend on the buying decision. If they can easily ascertain that an endcap offers a great value on some product, maybe they will buy the item. If it's totally unclear why the merchandise is there—or what is the purchase price—the consumer is going to walk right past that display.

Let's assume that the buyer has stacked the goods high in the stores and the signing is spectacular. The customers recognize a great value when they see it and they're purchasing boatloads of this product. It's a success. Now, what else can you sell to the consumer while they are in the store?

In department stores, so much kitchen equipment is bought indiscriminately by people who just come in for men's underwear.

Julia Child

I'm sure that you've heard the phrase "multiple sale," or devising ways to sell the customer several items during one shopping trip to a store. For example, if they were buying paper, a natural multiple sale would include a binder to hold the paper, some pens to write with, and manila folders. Typically, related articles are placed side by side on the selling floor to encourage more than one purchase. Pots and pans could have spatulas and potholders near by.

Retailers study the multiple purchasing habits of their customers through databases of information. When you pay for products at stores with savings cards, the cashier is recording all the items you've bought and forwarding that information to the retailer's giant database. If you came in to buy a portable CD player, what else did you buy? If most customers, in this example, also pick up blank CDR's (recordable compact discs), the retailer should be alerted to that trend. This is called an affinity—items that are purchased during the same transaction. An affinity could be a bag of dog food purchased with a dog food bowl. In men's clothing, an affinity might be a dress shirt and a tie.

Regardless of the type of merchandise being sold, by cleverly positioning affinities next to each other, you can drive multiple sales. I prefer to think of it this way: help the customer to be more satisfied with their purchase by offering them all related items as well. If they're buying hanging file folders, make certain that the hanging file folder tabs are sitting next to them on the shelf. If the customer makes a purchase and the affinities are not stationed nearby, the shopper might get home and realize that they needed other products to totally fill their requirements.

Product Presentation

Sales of merchandise clearly are impacted by the way the product is displayed on the selling floor. During my career, numerous vendors demanded that my buyers should place their merchandise in desirable locations—on endcaps, stacked on the selling floor or on a shelf at eye level. They were convinced that we'd kill their opportunities for sales otherwise. I found, however, that a presentation doesn't have to be big or on the perfect shelf to be effective. Experimenting with space, I learned that you could have a great selling item on the bottom shelf or hidden at the back of the store. Hopefully, you've had a few experiences like this too.

I came across an interesting article about this subject in an electronics magazine. They reported on an audio shop located in one of Japan's major cities. Like most large metropolitan areas, Japan's real estate is extremely expensive and retail stores sell their wares out of shoebox spaces. This hi-fi store had limited square footage, with speakers piled one on top of the other all the way up to the ceiling. Wires were running all over the selling floor. The place was a disaster area. Perhaps, you've been in a few stores that resemble this. When I encounter this "look," I usually turn and run back out the front door, fearing that I'll catch some rare disease.

This audio store is thriving, however, and is satisfying its customers. How do they do it? Well, they don't accomplish their goals with a great product presentation. They attract and keep their customers happy by offering a terrific assortment of products combined with great service. By marketing to the special needs of the demographics surrounding their store, the stereo shop connects tightly to their customers. They carry products that other stores refuse to stock.

The moral of the story: you should strive for the best presentation possible for your merchandise, but a great presentation doesn't guarantee great sales. I don't subscribe to the messy approach in merchandising. I do believe that presentation counts. But you do need to keep an open mind. If the buyer proposes an unorthodox layout for your goods, consider it. Short of the buyer sealing your stuff in a plain unmarked box and telling you "this will make your goods sell like hotcakes," try to trust your buyer's instincts.

Markdowns

Have you ever received a phone call from a frantic retail store buyer and the word "markdown" was part of the conversation? Is there any utterance more likely to wreak fear in the heart of a vendor? You do know why a buyer discusses markdowns with you, right? They want you to pay for it. (Well, the buyer wants you to pay for everything, but that's another story).

Who do you think owns the markdown? The answer: You do. Regardless of what's fair, or the fact that you did everything to insure the success of the merchandise, if the buyer wants you to pay for the markdown, don't they know the exact spot to press when exerting pressure on you? Sure, sometimes you can tell them "no," and some buyers occasionally accept it. But make no mistake, most buyers, and I'd throw in senior management at all retailers, expect the vendor to help fix the situation.

If an inventory nightmare requires a markdown, the retailer doesn't want it to eat into their profitability. They want you to pay for it. We can debate the fact that every expense imposed on the manufacturer probably finds a way back into the invoice prices of the merchandise. Fine, I understand that. But you won't get most buyers or top management at retailers to let you off the hook that easy. Bad inventory calls for either a markdown to move it or the ability to return it to the vendor. Face it, you don't want the goods back. So, if you can find it in your heart, and finances, get them a markdown quickly. That will qualify you as a good vendor.

Here, we are reinforcing the point that you are never off the hook after selling goods to retailers. I understand it's not fair, but if you know the buyer's underlying needs and plan accordingly, nothing should surprise you.

Should you volunteer to help? Certainly, that is honorable, if you can afford to do so. If you are stuck in a situation where eating a markdown would devastate you, can you offer some other alternative to the retailer? Can you provide the next shipment for free or come up with additional advertising dollars? When the buyer is stuck with products that have become a liability, it should have a positive impact if you can provide a solution.

What if the merchandise was a closeout? Even though suppliers stipulate that if you purchase a closeout it's your inventory for life, I have returned closeouts back to factories. You need to judge the severity of the situation. If your relationship with the buyer is at stake, or the buyer's reputation at their store is on shaky ground, try to find a way out of the problem. It is likely that the buyer will remember your good deed.

Rebates and incentives

For the uninitiated, rebates and incentives are monies given from the manufacturer back to the retailer as long as certain conditions are met. For example, a vendor could offer a 1% rebate for purchases of $500,000 and a 2% rebate for buying $750,000 annually. This type of rebate rewards the retailer if purchases increase. Other incentives could include monies available for coop advertising and discounts given for paying an invoice within a few days. Manufacturers intend for these funds to drive their businesses. The more the buyer purchases, the more rebate, advertising and other goodies can accrue.

How does a buyer look at rebates and incentive packages? Clearly, it depends on the retailer, but many retail buyers enjoy these programs. A few stores prefer to purchase their products "net-net," with all rebates, coop ad dollars and other incentives stripped out of the price. Experienced buyers understand that the cost for rebates, coop advertising and other incentives are built into the invoice price for the goods. The vendor is not giving the buyer the lowest price and then dipping deeply into their profitability to further enrich the buyer's bottom line. The cost is inflated to include rebate, coop, key market funds and more. Therefore, the consumer is paying for the retail store's incentive programs.

Here's an example: If the cost of an item was $5 and the buyer's margin goal was 50%, they'd sell it for $10. ($10 retail - $5 cost = $5. Then divide that $5 by the $10 retail = 50%). Let's suppose that loaded into that $5 cost was 2% rebate and 3% coop advertising. If this buyer chose to purchase without the incentives, the price would be $5 minus 5% or $4.75. In this case, a 50% margin would generate a $9.50 retail. So you can see that the incentive programs cost is passed on to the consumer with the $10 price.

Some vendors have gotten themselves into a world of pain because they didn't understand the incentive game. If a buyer asks for a net price—with coop, rebate, and other funny money removed—you must do some investigation. Does this store buy that way from all their suppliers? Do they have a way to fund their advertising through an internal budget? I've seen suppliers give buyers the best, "down and dirty" price, stripped of all extra funds, and then one month later the buyer runs an ad and bills the vendor. In this case, the vendor hasn't set any money aside for advertising—they sold the goods at a "net-net" price. The buyer is stuck because they don't have extra advertising monies; the vendor is really stuck because the buyer is probably going to ram this cost back to them. Typically, this is caused by a buyer's inexperience and poor communications skills—the new buyer. Your best protection here is to ask many questions before you give a price to the buyer.

Do you need an incentive program if you're planning on selling to retail stores? It depends on the retailer, but every department store, superstore and specialty store that employed me was hooked on incentives. Ask other vendors who are connected to a particular retailer. There are some extremely large retailers who don't want incentives. It's your job as a samurai salesperson to find out the specific needs of the buyer.

Do volume incentives grow business?

Any buyer in America would quickly answer "yes." They would tell you that a rebate encourages them to buy more merchandise, thereby generating an even higher rebate. But the reality is far more complex. Let's suppose that every vendor selling bed sheets had a rebate program and that the bottom line to the retailer was the same. If everything else was equal, no one vendor has an advantage.

However, these deals normally vary from vendor to vendor within a product category. If three manufacturers are selling the same product, each supplier usually will have a unique incentive package. Financially, one vendor's deal might be superior to another vendors. This might give an edge to one vendor. The buyer needs to compare the incentives between manufacturers, assess the quality of each vendor's product line and all the other factors needed for a quality business relationship. One supplier could have a better incentive program, but can't deliver the goods on time.

I have found that incentives do grow the business in most cases. However, if an extremely small vendor has an incentive, the payout to the retail store probably will be insignificant. That's not going to drive the buyer to increase purchases. Also, retailers are more cautious today about over buying to hit higher rebate levels—overstocking yourself with inventory, while you gain rebate dollars, doesn't always give you a return on the investment.

Incentives are an insurance policy for suppliers, keeping your competition at bay. How does that work? If everything is equal between vendors offering the same products—the merchandise quality, the service, the price and more are basically the same—but one vendor has more incentive dollars available for the retailer, that supplier is likely to get the business. Other vendors won't be considered until they are more competitive.

There are additional questions you need to ask about incentives:

Does a better rebate benefit the buyer's personal income?

Yes, rebates can benefit a buyer's personal income. In several chain stores, I was given rebate goals and hitting them enabled me to obtain a better annual review with a salary increase. If you are dealing with a buyer who has a similar arrangement, your rebate program can be even more effective in driving your sales. However, one place I worked didn't encourage the buyers to go after more rebate; consequently, we focused on other things. You need to research what motivates the buyer. Understand, nevertheless, that it is unlikely that the buyer will reveal to you how they're compensated. Perhaps, there are clever ways you can find that out.

Now let's ask a question again:

Do volume incentives grow business?

If a buyer has a choice between two suppliers with equal goods and identical service, and one vendor provides a larger volume incentive, who'd get the business? Based on the preceding paragraph, you can see that if the buyer is personally profiting from the agreement as well, won't they go after more rebate?

I realize that the most ethical members of the retail world will deny that incentive programs personally influence buyers. Buyers are supposed to rise above their personal needs and make independent decisions, the right judgment for their store. Of course, buyers are extremely concerned about their store's needs. But don't you think incentives can influence a buyer in other ways too. You be the judge.

Does the buyer get credit for the rebate or coop incentive?

The answer to the above question depends on the retailer. In many cases, both the rebate and coop achieved are part of a goal given to the buyer as part of their annual performance review. However, I did work for one retailer who was internally funded for coop advertising and didn't drive their buyers to get more from vendors. Know your customer and find out the answer, if possible.

Would you do more business by increasing your co-op fund?

Theoretically, if you have more coop funds available to the buyer, they should be able to advertise your product more, thereby increasing your sales, right? That is true. But if you're a small vendor, you might not be able to afford running an ad. More ad dollars wouldn't accomplish anything in that scenario. Yet, in most cases, yes, the more coop advertising monies offered to them, the more you are likely to grow your business. This question should be easy for a buyer to answer. Understand that most buyers will tell you to immediately increase your ad funds to them—they're encouraged to get more and more out of you. Find out how they will utilize the funds before you open your wallet.

Merrill's favorite question not asked by salespeople:

Do you know what that question is?

How is the product selling?

Isn't that a wonderful question? It's succinct, yet to the point. This question implies that you care about the product's sales. That also means that you care about the buyer's business. Doesn't this question make you feel all warm inside? I know that it always impressed me when a supplier asked the question—a total of maybe 5 times in my career.

Here's the point: Salespeople rarely ask how a product is performing. Have all sales folks been programmed only to sell? That little question, above, is part of the follow up, and isn't that a critical part of being a great salesperson today? Of course it is important. But, trust me, very few people ask the question. If you intelligently ask the question, it will show that you are a true partner to the buyer.

Here's how you shouldn't ask the question: "How did the product sell?"

Here's a superior way to pose it: "Say, two months ago I sold you 25% more of product X than we've been trending for the past year. That was a great purchase, and I was glad to sell it to you. But did the ad you ran bring in the customers? Were your sales higher than usual? Did the ad results meet your expectations?"

The buyer is acutely concerned with the sales of their products and the generation of a profit. If merchandise is not ringing in the register, the goods are useless. Show the buyer that you care about their business and aren't merely there to shovel goods down the pipeline. Ask them the question, please, and make me very happy.

There are other questions that you need to ask—and get the answers too. Do you know how your products are turning? Are your goods selling but the retailer owns too much inventory? Are other retailers selling more of this product?

Can you help the buyer to sell more goods? Is there a way to support the buyer by providing training to store associates and product presentations to customers? Are you able to alert the buyer or inventory manager to out of stocks?

Could you volunteer to take back the worst sellers? I always told my suppliers that their merchandise occupied their space on the sales floor. If their area contained bad sellers, they were underutilizing their space. However, I'd add, if they replaced the weak merchandise with better goods, it would be beneficial for both of us. Think about it.

Packaging

You can read entire textbooks on the importance of proper packaging and how it attracts consumers to products. When you compare the packaging from 20 years ago to designs on store shelves today, it's almost amusing, as if we were in the dark ages back then. Effective packaging has grown substantially, developing into an art form in some cases. If you are doing business with moderate to larger retailers in America today, it is critical that you have your product surrounded by a distinctive, attractive and well-designed package.

Perhaps you've heard the phrase, "silent salesperson." Retail stores don't have salespeople waiting for customers in every aisle. When you are shopping in a mega-store and can't find a product, don't you love having to grab a roaming store associate, who quickly tells you that they can't answer any of your questions, and then proceeds to page for backup help via the public address system? The personal treatment is alive and well in the larger stores. With quality packaging, serving as a silent salesperson, the features and benefits of your merchandise can be emblazoned across the box, thereby helping the consumer to understand the contents.

I've watched countless shoppers in retail stores. Folks cruise through aisles or past fixtures, and some of the merchandise and presentations "talk" to the consumer. Think about it. When you are in a store, what attracts your attention and why? Is there a reason that you walk past some items, yet stop to evaluate other products? What drives impulse purchases? How long does a customer pause while examining a product? The consumer will spend about one nanosecond with merchandise before they move on.

If shoppers are "on a mission," with limited time, and they are rushing into the store to buy something specifically, they may tune out all the other products competing for their attention. However, if they are browsing, retailers utilize all kinds of presentation techniques to pull in the consumer. Good packaging should do that as well and aid in the completion of the sale.

Suppliers who offer superlative packaging to their retail buyers have a major advantage over their competition. An entire merchandise category can be imbued with life as a result of a packaging change. I've experienced sales increases ranging from 5% to more than 50% due to a packaging improvement. Here's the disclaimer: "Not all packaging changes are guaranteed these results. Your actual outcome may vary substantially." I've seen new packaging bomb too. But if you test your packaging on the public and ask your buyers for input, you might create something truly wonderful.

Buyers today are critically analyzing your packaging because they know that it helps to drive sales. If the buyer can't quickly ascertain what's in the box or package, how would they expect the consumer to do so? Great packaging has "beauty shots" on the cover in full color, with "bullet points," or markings that emphasize important features of the product. Superior packaging grabs, attracts, explains and answers any question the consumer may have about the goods.

I worked for one retail organization that called me the "professor of packaging," because I devoutly believe in its importance. In one industry, I took sorry looking white and red boxed items and completely gutted that image, moving to sexy, full color designs with bullet points. My sales increased nicely. I've been involved with the redesign of packaging for complicated, multi-featured electronic merchandise as well. In every case, store associates were thrilled because the product's details were easy to read on the cover of the box and it helped them to complete sales. Also, the consumer was able to connect with the message: "I am a quality product that has these features and benefits, and I'd like you to buy me."

Be prepared for today's buyer to ask you about your packaging. If they're sniffing around and questioning you about "how attached are you to your packaging," they're wondering if you're willing to improve it with their assistance. More than likely, they can conceive of a better way to sell your merchandise, and you should listen to their concepts with an open mind. Sure, I understand that packaging costs money and, if you've spent a small fortune on the development of your existing design, it's painful to make a significant change. But you need to recognize that buyers are on the front lines with the retail store associates and the end user, the consumer. Buyers often know what sells and what doesn't. Pay attention to them and perhaps your packaging will become more magnificent with their support. The worst thing that could happen is that you might sell more merchandise.

Imports

How do buyers look at imports and how can this impact the sales professional? Most industries today have some level of competition from imported goods. Unless a store staunchly is devoted to domestic products, you will find that many buyers are encouraged by their management to grow their import merchandise assortment. The reasons are simple—profitability. Assuming that the quality of the imported goods equal domestic products, the Far East, Mexico, South America, India and other parts of the world are able to manufacture items for less money. Entire industries have moved "offshore" for a variety of reasons including lower labor costs; take the consumer electronics business, for example.

Today, you are competing with manufacturers from all over the globe. Is your product something that could be produced overseas for less money? Can the basic concept be copied, or do you have the design and features legally protected? You need to be aware that buyers are under the gun to increase their profits to the corporation, and one way is to grow their import private label (store brand) business. If your merchandise is a commodity, and many factories are cranking out identical items, could production of this product be taken overseas?

The message here is that you need to watch your back. If the buyer is happy with the quality of goods, service, pricing and all the other things that contribute to a great relationship, they might not be inclined to ship your idea to a foreign factory. But if your product isn't unique, your service stinks and your competition offers a better price, should the retailer create their own version of your goods with their brand name on the box? Would you impel them to import a similar item?

I've represented several large chain stores and each one had the resources to buy container loads of imported goods. The impetus was there—buying in quantity from overseas saved us a ton of money vs. the domestic version.

Should your factory contemplate shifting some of its business overseas? Certainly, if you are under intense price competition, it is a consideration. I've seen many organizations segment their business, shifting some categories offshore, and continuing to specialize in other products in the USA.

Opportunities for foreign suppliers contacting retailers can vary from industry to industry. Booths of imported goods are visible at every American tradeshow, regardless of the industry. The buyers do have access to these vendors.

You, the samurai salesperson, should be aware of your import competition and how they're going to market. You also must develop a strategy for dealing with them. Don't wait for trouble to appear; anticipate how imports could impact your current business now and keep your eyes open for future encroachment from these factories.

Chapter 13

Rules and Regulations

THOUGHT #12

Arresting shadows is something you do when adversaries' aggressive intentions toward you are perceptible. ...This means to arrest the enemy's action at the point of the very impulse to act. If you demonstrate strongly to opponents how you control the advantage, they will change their minds, inhibited by this strength.[10]

Miyamoto Musashi

Musashi is brilliant on this particular quote; but I do enjoy them all. What a terrific strategy to take with your competition! Suppose you had heard that a competing factory was working on a new product. What if your company indicated that you were preparing to launch a similar item immediately? Would your competition lay down its cards and reveal its strategy to their retail customers? I've known a few organizations out there that utilize tactics like this and it has worked for them. But this strategy is not for the weak of heart.

Military battle plans and business both can be relentless in the pursuit of their goals, and winners are resolute. Yet, the military or business worlds abide by rules that guide their direction. These rules provide structure and management of the personnel, detailing acceptable and improper behavior. Let's talk about business rules that impact the buyer and the salesperson.

In this chapter, we'll discuss social etiquette between buyers and sellers; putting things in writing; unauthorized deductions and accounts payable; meetings with buyers; and retail law.

Social Etiquette

In the business world, there is acceptable and unacceptable behavior. Whereas some salespeople were telling tall sexual tales twenty years ago, this is not permissible today. There is a well-defined line in the sand concerning behavior in business and you'd best not cross it. You may sell sexy merchandise, but you may not employ sexy comments. The retail samurai salesperson is extremely cautious in their approach to a customer through words and actions. Even if you do not *intend* your words to offend anyone or put them on their guard, the critical point is *how your comments were interpreted.* It's a fine line between clever conversation and something construed as threatening, harassing or discriminating. I've attended many human resource (HR) seminars on proper behavior and HR experts will tell you, if the other party feels discriminated against or is uncomfortable with your words or deeds, your style and professionalism will be questioned, and you could be opening yourself and your company to a world of pain (like lawsuits).

Human resource folks will recommend against jokes with sexual innuendos, graphic language and cursing. I'd add to that list jokes dealing with religion and politics. You don't really know exactly how another human being is going to interpret your words, and sex or religion or politics are potential landmines. Why risk your reputation for a laugh?

Many of you have heard about sexual harassment. I can tell you that this does occur when men are taking advantage of women, especially in a subordinate role, but this can take place between a buyer and seller as well. Comments or even physical acts can be misunderstood. Are you a "touch-y feel-y" type of person? You express yourself verbally and enhance your comments with occasional gentle touches to the other person who is part of the conversation? What if they don't like being touched? What if you're not careful *where* you are touching them? If you're a man and are touching a woman customer, how do they know what your touching is leading to? This is dangerous ground for a salesperson.

Sexual harassment is not only taking place in the corporate world; it also can happen between a male salesperson and female buyer. It can occur between a female salesperson and male buyer too. One male buyer that I knew was in a very difficult situation when a female salesperson utilized wily tactics with him: she mixed her sales presentation with suggestive comments and physical actions that led to a very uncomfortable position for this man. She would talk to him freely about her sexual exploits and often pointed to parts of her body, asking the buyer if he admired them. Management ultimately confronted the female salesperson.

Even if you've known the buyer for many years, it doesn't excuse unprofessional conduct. The best rule to follow here is to take the high road all the time. Do nothing that could be interpreted as a sexual advance.

Salespeople have to be careful of many other things in their relationships with buyers. It's fun to shower your favorite buyers with gifts, especially during holidays and their birthdays, but you must be mindful of how your graciousness will be perceived. I've been handed $500 leather winter jackets, expensive clocks and other wonderful things, but I never kept them. It was inappropriate. Why do sellers provide gifts to their buyers? "They're friends and business partners of mine." Sure they are. I'm certain that you'd be their best buddies if you had no business reasons, right?

Buyers beware! Many retail organizations today have extremely strict policies concerning gifts, meals or accepting anything from a salesperson. Some large stores have been known for refusing to permit buyers to receive even a cup of coffee from a supplier. Can you understand why? You are unfairly trying to influence the buyer when you provide gifts. Buyers are encouraged to remain objective in their judgment of products, and suppliers and gifts can be perceived as bribes or payoffs or something unethical. Do you want to be viewed in this light? Around holiday times, many retailers issue a statement to their suppliers regarding gift giving. The more liberal stores will prefer for suppliers, who feel compelled to give gifts, to send fruit baskets or chocolates that can be consumed by the buying office. Conservative stores don't want you to give presents at all. You must familiarize yourselves with the retailer's corporate policy so you don't break their rules.

What about drinking with your buyers? How about the sharing of any other substance? Again, this is a difficult road to walk. A casual cocktail or beer doesn't seem very harmful, but you must know your customer. How will the buyer or their management perceive such behavior? Camaraderie with business associates often includes a drink at a restaurant or bar, so I encourage you to use your best judgment. On the other hand, any other substances should be avoided like the plague. It is not cool to offer a buyer any type of drug, in any form whatsoever. You can be accused of substance abuse and that's a terrible moniker to remove from your record.

When I was an assistant buyer, I faced my first sales person bearing gifts at holiday times. Certainly, he was out to manipulate the buyers. We were given lots of drinks during our meals together. One time, after a heavy holiday restaurant feast, he motioned us out to his Cadillac in the parking lot and hoisted full bottles of whiskey out of his car trunk as gifts. I was very uncomfortable with the entire proceeding, but he demanded that we accept the bottles as "tokens of his appreciation." He put me in a difficult position. I wasn't looking to offend him, yet I was highly concerned about how the episode would look to my management. As a result, I told them about the gift. This salesman was devious. It was a horrible way to conduct business. Is that the way you want people to think of you? Will the retail management become unhappy with you? There are better ways of working with buyers.

Putting Things In Writing

Don't buyers forget and lose everything? I'm sure that many salespeople believe that it's intentional and in some cases that can be true. Remember what you learned in the early chapters of this book: buyers are very busy and get lots of email and correspondence. You aren't the only person in their life. They are juggling lots of balls and are struggling to keep them up in the air.

Save everything that you send to the buyer or discuss with them—projections, comments, emails. If you had a positive conversation, document it. If you can send a copy of a letter or email to the buyer's superior, you should. However, if that will be perceived as "going over my head," or "unnecessarily involving my boss," then don't do it.

I have witnessed many well-intentioned salespeople who didn't put the contents of a conversation in writing and lived to suffer the consequences. For example, suppose that buyers quit their jobs or move elsewhere within the retail organization. Will their successor abide by their commitments to you? If you don't have something in writing, you might have trouble executing the previous plan. Formulating a large product rollout? Did you bother to involve the buyer's boss in some way, even to mention your appreciation for the future business? Guess what happens if you don't? Everyone gets executive amnesia, just like a really bad TV movie plot. The previous buyer was bonked on the head and everything has become really fuzzy. "I never agreed to that." Ever hear those words before? Wait a second! I used to say that.

To be fair, amnesia victims include both buyers and salespeople. It's very convenient. A new buyer coming into an assignment, especially a buyer afflicted with new buyer-itis, has their hands full, learning a new area and more. They want to create their own kingdom with their handpicked vendors. Good luck if you didn't document anything and if you kept the retailer's management in the dark. New buyers also encounter shrewd salespeople who offer all kinds of outlandish claims. "The last buyer firmly committed to us that they'd buy this product and, based on their comments, we've built the inventory and are ready to ship it to you." Although outgoing buyers may not communicate properly to those who follow, I'm sure that salespeople utilize the change in management to their advantage as well. If you don't want to be declared a scoundrel, keep great records of all your interactions with the buyers.

Unauthorized Deductions and Accounts Payable

I speak in front of groups of salespeople, many who firmly believe that the accounts payable (AP) departments of retailers like to obfuscate the truth and lengthen the payment process. Yes, strange things do seem to occur in the accounting area, but is that hard to understand? They're accountants and converse in a different language than buyers and sellers. Although we all utilize numbers, AP clerks are involved with lots more paper and numbers than most business people. Are they acting in the best interests of their employer? Of course they are. I do not believe that AP departments are doing anything underhanded or that they are attempting to withhold payments from their suppliers. Yet, they do seem to come from another planet sometimes.

When the going gets tough with the money your company is owed, should you ask for the buyer's support? Yes, you can involve the buyer only if that is their preference. Many buyers are so busy that a trip to accounting is like impaling themselves on a steel rod. You need to find out what your buyer desires. Some folks like to have their hands on everything that touches their areas of responsibility. Other buyers would prefer to delegate as much as possible.

Regardless, you must have a relationship with the accounts payable manager. Don't wait for a problem to first occur before you introduce yourself. If your buyer approves of your direct relationship with AP, the payables manager will be a lifesaver for you. For many buyers, if you can't resolve problems with AP, then, and only then, would they encourage you to ask for their assistance.

The best salespeople fix AP issues so the buyer doesn't need to be involved. However, if an AP deduction or calculation will lead to the vendor putting the retailer on credit hold, you need to step in and intercede. There are many reasons why an invoice might not have been fully paid. But you shouldn't let the factory cut off shipments to the retailer. There is nothing more infuriating to a buyer than finding out that they're not receiving goods due to an accounting dispute. "You're not paying us properly. We haven't received a check on time, so we're not shipping until we get payment." This is especially nasty for buyers who have placed expected merchandise into an ad and then they awake to a catastrophic problem—the ad is in the newspaper, but the goods never arrived at the stores due to an accounting debacle.

Accounts payable issues tie into the concept of positive confrontation. Let your buyer know that, "I've attempted to solve this problem with AP, but I need your help."

Meetings

The samurai salesperson must pay attention to their environment and all events taking place around them. They are poised, always ready to assist the buyer, helping to bring projects to their conclusion. As a samurai salesperson, you also need to be considerate. Even though it may take you weeks or months to receive an audience with the highly esteemed buyer, resist the temptation to overstay your visit. If you schedule a meeting with a buyer, do them a favor and come to the party with a plan and an agenda, and keep the session as short as possible.

Buyers go to innumerable meetings, and your time with them is one of many meetings. Try to keep to 30-60 minutes, if possible. Be conscious of time that you are using. Every minute with you takes them away from the rest of their responsibilities. So, it is gratifying if they're giving you plenty of attention, but you still should show your consideration by keeping your meeting flowing, on schedule and sticking to the topic.

They'll appreciate your efforts.

Retail Law

Please keep your attorney jokes to yourself. I don't profess to be a lawyer, yet I've attended many classes on retail law and have taught the subject as well. Also, I've been fortunate to discuss retail law in detail with attorneys who were highly knowledgeable. They told me that any company or person who violates either of the Acts mentioned below is eligible for a multi-million dollar fine and other horrible problems.

If you'd like to continue being a salesperson, you need to be aware of the fact that there are federal laws on the books that concern retailers and people who sell to them. Ignorance is no excuse to the federal government. Violate the law and they'd be happy to provide daily meals and housing in a secured facility that is lacking a golf course. Essentially, the government wants to insure that the consumer gets a fair deal in the marketplace and that no one is conspiring to control retail prices or preventing a smooth flow of goods.

When I was a new buyer with Federated Department Stores, they provided a very effective movie for their buying team to view concerning retail law. You don't forget these types of films. It showed retail buyers and manufacturers being led away in handcuffs, on their way to prison, for violation of federal laws.

There are two significant pieces of legislation on the books: the **Sherman Anti-Trust Act** and the **Robinson Patman Act**. The retail environment in the 1920's and 1930's must have resembled the Wild West frontier days of the USA. Bad guys were roaming the plains and encouraged business people to do all kinds of unethical things.

The Sherman Anti-Trust Act was passed first in the 1920's, and its goal was to drive competition in the marketplace and to maintain free enterprise. In the 1930's, an additional group of laws were passed—the Robinson Patman Act—seeking to provide equal treatment to all buyers.

The retail environment in the 20's and 30's had widespread iniquities in the marketplace. Large stores were exerting their influence on suppliers, forcing them to provide significantly lower invoice prices. Some retailers weren't happy with their competition and encouraged vendors to stop shipping them. Can you imagine that? You're a retail buyer and your competition gets you upset, so you tell a supplier to stop shipping your competition. In other instances, competing retailers would conspire to maintain the same prices in all their stores. Also, manufacturers would dictate retail prices to the stores they sold. They were really troubling times.

In stepped the Federal government and they weren't happy with the landscape. The Sherman Anti-Trust Act identified unscrupulous, and illegal, business activity. Competing stores were no longer allowed to agree to the same selling prices on items. Competitors were not permitted to pass pricing information between themselves. **"Price fixing"** became an illegal activity. If competitors agreed to set a specific price on merchandise, or if they exchanged information between themselves about their prices, this was considered to be "horizontal" price fixing. If information was disseminated between manufacturers and retailers that constituted an agreement to precise retail pricing, this was "vertical" price fixing.

The Sherman Anti-Trust Act permitted manufacturers to sell to whomever they wanted. *Suggested* retail pricing was acceptable. However, the vendor was forbidden to *dictate* what the selling price should be.

The Robinson Patman Act covered other retailer/vendor issues. It forbade the selling of goods at lower prices to one store vs. another store unless there were certain conditions present. Let's suppose that competing stores were very similar in sales volume and the type of customers they attracted. A factory couldn't legally sell the same item to both stores and give a lower price to one of the stores. If the products offered to two retailers were similar, but not identical, there could be a different invoice price. If there were lower expenses involved doing business with one retailer vs. another, the seller could pass a cost savings on to that retailer. For example, if one retailer had a warehouse and another retail chain required shipping to individual stores, there were increased costs to the factory for transporting goods to multiple locations. The retailer with a warehouse could be offered a lower price. You also could justify a lower cost if one store was buying significantly larger quantities than another.

Here are some things you don't want to do, because you will be in violation of US law:

1) Selling to a buyer at a different price than the rest of the world without any justification.
2) Encouraging a retailer to set a specific retail price.
3) Giving buyers merchandise on an exclusive basis without the retailer doing something significant to deserve such treatment.

For example, if they bought your entire inventory or helped you to create merchandise, then there is justification.

4) Asking a buyer for pricing information and passing that information to their competition.

5) Taking a suggestion from a buyer that you stop selling to their competition.

It's easier than you think to violate the law. Suppose that you mentioned to one of your buyers that they were priced too high on an item. The week before you had visited their competition and had been told that their competition was lowering prices to $9.99 on some merchandise. You pass that information to your customer. What's wrong with that? "Hey, I'm innocent. I didn't force the retailer to set a specific retail price." You are dead wrong. You were **serving as a conduit of information** and forwarding intelligence to another store. Even though they weren't in collusion, you were aiding the process. You can suggest retails, but no more. When I encountered manufacturers who weren't too savvy and didn't know the law, I'd say the following disclaimer: "I appreciate your suggestions. But it's up to me to set my retails, independently, based on market conditions and the margin strategy of my corporation."

Buyers who exert undo influence on your prices, without providing good reasons for doing so, also can put your business in jeopardy. I was speaking with a director of a major corporation that was struggling with this situation. He sold goods to two competing retailers. However, the smaller volume retailer was requesting significant price and financial incentives, a deal that was better than what was given to the larger retailer. If you're stuck in this situation, can you ask the retailer to provide some additional benefits to your business? They could add more skus of merchandise than their competition, advertise more frequently, provide special sales training to their store associates, or more.

The buyer constantly will challenge you for special treatment and, if you provide it, you'll be in violation of the law. Retail buyers are notorious for complaining about their competition. Buyers have experienced their competition "crushing" the retail price of a perfectly profitable sku. Typically, the buyer learns that this great product is selling at an unconscionable profit margin when their competition puts this item into a published advertisement. Retail buyers of extremely promotional merchandise, like electronics, ride a roller coaster. Their nightmare begins when the competitor has bastardized the price of a great item, and that product will appear in an ad for the buyer's store within days, locked in print at a higher price. The management of most retail stores will then encourage the buyer to pick up the phone and raise hell with the vendor who sold the merchandise to both stores.

In a perfect world, the vendor should have developed an advertising strategy with each store that avoided a headlong confrontation. However, retailers can independently adjust their advertising, with the intent of embarrassing their competition. Regardless, the vendor gets blamed. If you are encouraged to stop shipping the offending retailer because it is hacking off your other customer, you can't do that. It's called **restraint of trade**. If the buyer asks you to "manage" the other retailer, what exactly can you legally do? Are you going to tell the offending store to run a higher retail price? You can't do that either. The smart samurai salesperson takes the abuse from the buyer and tries to find a way to prevent such awkward situations in the future. Perhaps, you can find some other way to make the buyer happy—but keep it legal and ethical.

There's so much more involved in these two Acts, that it would require another book to fully cover all the details. This is a case of "what you don't know can hurt you." For additional information, please contact attorneys specializing in these affairs, read about these laws online or in a library, or talk with an experienced retail samurai merchant or salesperson.

Chapter 14
Knocking Out Your Competition

THOUGHT #13

If you are concerned with the strength of your sword, you will try to cut unreasonably strongly, and will not be able to cut at all.... If you rely on strength, when you hit the enemy's sword you will inevitably hit too hard. If you do this, your own sword will be carried along as a result. Thus the saying, "The strongest hand wins," has no meaning. In large-scale strategy, if you have a strong army and are relying on strength to win, but the enemy also has a strong army, the battle will be fierce.... The spirit of my school is to win through the wisdom of strategy, paying no attention to trifles. Study this well.[11]

Mïyamoto Musashi

Musashi's point is that strength alone won't win a battle. Instead, he takes the higher path, choosing to beat his adversary through acumen and carefully crafted campaigns. This is a road that taps into intellect vs. brute strength. Your competitive struggles should incorporate this thinking. In all of my experiences, the large companies that threw their weight around, intimidating smaller players, were never as respected as the corporations that followed their own course, confident in their own direction. Industry leaders don't need to criticize other players and point out their shortcomings; instead, they can impress you with their accomplishments, level of organization, and the quality of their products and services. Leaders walk the higher road and knock out their competition through more clever means.

Make Yourself Invaluable to the Buyer

When retailers rate their suppliers, the best of the best have found this formula to be invaluable to the buyer. In chapter 9, we talked about how a buyer looks at their vendors and the six critical elements necessary for the buyer to classify you as a great business partner. These components set you apart from all the other peddlers out there. Do you remember what was required?

111

1) Quality products with terrific packaging
2) Delivered on time and backed by superior service
3) Competitively priced
4) Outstanding communication
5) Cutting edge merchandise that leads the industry and reinvents the category
6) Profitability—the buyer can make money on your products

If your organization has mastered the six factors above, you are walking an enlightened path, and you should be classified as a leader, an invaluable business associate. Although you might believe that many companies successfully accomplish the six items above, sadly, this isn't the case. It isn't easy to be a master.

In business, it is common to classify the buyer/seller relationship as a **partnership**, with each organization gaining from the interaction. The partnership word once meant that two or more people were contractually or legally bound, possibly co-owners of a business. Today, the word has been loosely assigned to anyone doing business together. Well, if some stores call their customers "guests," I suppose there's nothing wrong calling a retailer and its suppliers "a partnership." To me, the partnership word is grossly overused. I believe that a partnership needs to be defined by the six qualities stated above, demonstrating a relationship that is firing on all cylinders, a *dynamic* relationship. If the business association isn't achieving those things, it shouldn't be considered a partnership; it's merely buyers and sellers. There should be nothing common about a partnership. If you evaluated your current relationships, I would hope that you could think of a few true partnerships.

Some organizations transcend the above experiences and rise beyond a partnership to an even higher level of achievement, called a **strategic alliance**. In this pact, two organizations are joined at the hip, working closely together, sharing intimate information, and talking openly about any topic, with thoughts flowing seamlessly between all levels of each company. The bond between the two companies is cemented by trust and understanding. Each side is devoutly dedicated to success for the other party. When problems arise, as they inevitably will, there is a team focused on solving it. The word "no" doesn't exist in the vocabulary of either firm; instead a spirit of winning, growth and problem solving is deeply ingrained in the participants. There is no fear and "opening the kimono" is done gracefully. You are in business with soul mates, strategic thinkers who share the same concepts, ideals and desires; two companies joined together to travel down the path towards greater profits and stronger businesses. It's also not surprising that companies engaged in strategic alliances seem to have a lot of fun working together.

As we talk about the ultimate relationships available to you, are you re-evaluating the status of your business partners? How would you categorize your connections with your customers? Are they mediocre, hanging by a thread? Do you have a pretty good level of interactivity taking place, and you'd call them partners? Or have you risen beyond the mundane existence of most buyers and sellers? Does your relationship with one of your customers qualify for strategic alliance status? As Musashi said above, it's not strength that helps you to win; it's wisdom and strategy.

If you are a successful salesperson—if you're a retail samurai salesperson—it has to be tied to the quality of your relationships. You have nurtured your accounts, growing them slowly, tending to their needs, like a good gardener cultivates his crops, until the business sprouts, rises, expands and matures into something larger, grander. You conceived of something much more wonderful in the beginning. Your deft hand took a seed, a mere kernel, nothing more than a thought, and developed it into something living, breathing, vibrant, with legs—a thriving business. You should be proud of your accomplishments! It is not easy to start a business relationship and raise it to the heavens.

Still, samurai salespeople constantly are analyzing the status of their businesses, where they stand with their customers. You need to ask yourself if you are satisfied in your dealings with the retail buyer. If not, what are you doing wrong?

Do you think like a merchant? Or have you been approaching the buyer as one more peddler?

Do you have a relationship with senior management for your customer? Do you know the inventory manager, rebuyer, assistant buyer and buyers from other departments within the retailer's corporation? What's the quality of communication between your customer service department and the buyer's store associates? Do your order entry people treat the customer with respect and assist them rapidly when needed? You regularly talk with the buyer, but can the buyer reach your boss? Can the merchandise manager speak with your boss or your president? Does top management at your company ever talk with the president of the retailer? In short, can information flow easily between your two companies? If not, you have a hill that you need to climb. It is critical to your success as a salesperson and important to the longevity of your business relationships.

What Are the 10 Qualities of the Best Salespeople?

At my full day seminars, we review the six critical elements necessary for the buyer to classify you as a great business partner, listed in Chapter 9 and earlier in this chapter. Then, I have some fun with the salespeople in the audience. "Do you know the ten qualities of the best salespeople," I ask them. Invariably, I receive about four to five great answers from the crowd. I remind them that I am the samurai warrior buyer, and this top ten list is based on the viewpoint of retail buyers. How would a retail buyer enumerate the best qualities of the salespeople who call on them? If you emulate these qualities, you will be considered a superior salesperson.

1) **Best lines of merchandise.** If you don't have the goods, how good are you? As we've discussed, you must represent quality items that have features and benefits to solve consumer needs.

2) **Anticipate problems before they occur so the buyer doesn't need to get involved.** Remember that the buyer doesn't have time to fool around with merchandise issues; they barely have time to do their jobs. Keep things flowing smoothly and you'll be their hero.

3) **Handle problems lightning fast when they occur.** Why would your company need you if problems never reared their ugly heads? Salespeople are problem solvers and you should be proud of that fact. Let the buyer know how you fixed a nightmare and move on. They'll be glad to know you.

4) **You are cordial.** With stress and constant complications, the buyer needs a friendly voice and face in the wilderness. Even if the buyer puts you under the gun, rise above the intensity, stay professional and be nice.

5) **Show intelligence.** Most buyers are pretty savvy businesspeople and are intelligent. They like to surround themselves with similar minded folks. Show them your wisdom, patience and brilliance. Use your cranium to help them to drive their business with you.

6) **Walk the line.** You must fight for the viewpoint of your customer. You must totally understand the way the buyer thinks and represent their ideology back to your headquarters. Isn't that one of your primary responsibilities? You are the eyes and ears of your corporation and you forward information about your territory and your customers. How are the products selling? What does the buyer think? Even though your paycheck has the manufacturer's name on it, you must walk the line and

fight for the buyer's point of view. If you are angering your management by telling them that their ideas won't satisfy your customer, you are walking the line. If you notify your boss that a strategy won't work, and your boss says, "stop taking the buyer's point of view," you are walking the line. If your boss snidely asks, "whose name is on your paycheck?" You are walking the line. At that point, you can pat yourself hard on the back. You have represented your customer's feelings. Let the buyer know that you are fighting battles—and hopefully winning them—for the buyer's interests. That will make you a true business partner. Think like a merchant or forever be a peddler. When you walk the line, you have become the merchant!! Excellent! Be careful, however. Walking the line means that you have to listen to your boss, too. If you only push for the buyer's point of view and never reflect the position of your company, you can risk the brand of insubordination. Walk the line cautiously and don't fall off.

7) **Have a supportive office staff.** Isn't it amazing how many phone calls are required, the quantity of paperwork and all the time necessary to complete a project? Whether you have folks backing you up in an office down the street from your customer, or the support team is clear across the country at your corporate headquarters, a crew backing your mission is a requirement for success. You may cut through layers of bureaucracy and accomplish great feats of strength by yourself, but you need other people to help you fully complete your tasks.

8) **Helps the buyer with their paperwork** (and anything else that will speed the process up). Many salespeople complain about this item when I mention it. "Why do I need to do the buyer's job for them?" "It's not my paperwork!" "If I do paperwork for them, what else will they unload on me?" "I've been doing the buyer's paperwork, but they're taking advantage of me and I need to break them of the habit." I have heard all the issues concerning this one. In a perfect world, you wouldn't need to help the buyer to complete their jobs. In that idyllic universe, all nations on the planet respect one another, and buyer's offices have enough staff to complete their workloads. WAKE UP!! Come back down to earth! How can you help the buyer? If they're juggling a million glass balls of responsibility and, if one ball drops it will break into a million smaller shards of glass, their eyes are locked on the sky and they can't let anything fall. You are only one of the balls aloft. Let that fact

humble you. The retail samurai salesperson does whatever is necessary to complete the sale of the product, even if that means filling out paperwork, talking with the buyer's display department, visiting store operations or schmoozing with the buyer's boss. There's no shame in completing the process, but it's totally unrewarding if your merchandise isn't added to their assortment because you didn't want to help. When there are no purchase orders, there are no commission checks—and that is not an ancient Oriental saying.

9) **Tell the best jokes.** Come on!! Yes, I'm serious. The best salespeople also have the best entertainment material. It's a jungle out there, and buyers need a little respite from it all. I still remember some of the jokes one of my first salespeople told me. Oops! I can't relay them to you. They're no longer politically correct. A sense of humor does go a long way in business. Everyone is rushing here and there—pulling 10-14 hour days—and a kind, smiling face that relays something amusing is manna from heaven.

10) **Know the best restaurants for lunch.** Well, even buyers who can't laugh know how to eat, so number ten is really important. Some of the best relationships can be built over a good meal. Everyone is relaxed. Put some food into their stomachs, and watch them confess all their sins. Gastronomic delights are like truth serum; a full belly mellows out folks, stripping away the outer barriers to our personalities. Besides all that, you probably will take the buyer out to a more expensive restaurant than they would normally visit on their own time. It can make for a very special shared moment.

So that's the top ten qualities for the best salespeople. These qualities are all extremely meaningful to most buyers, and if you practice all ten of them, you're probably a very successful retail samurai salesperson today.

Samurai salespeople set themselves apart from their competition and think like merchants. Buyers consider you a consummate professional. Practice all these principles and you will knock out your competition. Isn't that the way you want to be remembered?

Chapter 15

Other Valuable Information You Need to Know (Or Else)

THOUGHT #14

Stance in Strategy. Adopt a stance with the head erect, neither hanging down, nor looking up, nor twisted. Your forehead and the space between your eyes should not be wrinkled. Do not roll your eyes nor allow them to blink, but slightly narrow them.... In all forms of strategy, it is necessary to maintain the combat stance in everyday life and to make your everyday stance your combat stance. You must research this well.[12]

Miyamoto Musashi

Are you ready for any obstacle that can be thrown in your path? Have you fully researched your customer, the buyer, and have adopted the appropriate mindset? Are you mentally ready to face the buyer and win? Does your body language reflect Musashi's "stance in strategy?"

We have talked about detailed preparation and the understanding that is required to succeed when you are facing down the gatekeeper—the buyer. But there are a few other details that you must know. As Musashi has said, you cannot overlook anything.

Can You Fix a Sick Category with a Change to the Assortment?

Yes. The best retail stores are constantly reinventing themselves, changing their presentations and mix of merchandise. If your buyer is faced with a deteriorating business—if it is sick—you can make it healthier by deeply examining the assortment and making precision-like changes where necessary. Can you assist the buyer, take back or mark down bad sellers, and make room for your newer, and better, merchandise?

Should You Ever Surprise a Buyer at a Tradeshow?

Typically, buyers are wary of surprises, especially ones at tradeshows. Are you revealing new products at a show and don't want any of your customers to see the goods before the unveiling? You're looking for a dramatic entrance? That is a dangerous approach, especially with buyers from larger chain stores. It's their job to know what is happening in the marketplace, and that includes new item rollouts. If you choose to ignore the role they play within their corporation, serving as the most knowledgeable person running a category, you will embarrass them in front of their management.

Your best customers need to either view the new products in special ceremonies you plan, or you must schedule time at the tradeshow for them to "be among the first to see" these great new items. It is the worst feeling in the world for a buyer to stop at an existing vendor's booth at a tradeshow, and there is new merchandise sitting on the table—and the buyer has never seen it, and their management is standing beside them.

Buyers and their management often walk the aisles of tradeshows, and they discuss business needs, all the while looking for the next great product that will drive their sales. This is the buyer's opportunity to show their connections to the manufacturing community and their deep understanding of their business. You will damage their standing with their management if they're not in sync with your new item plans. At your tradeshow booth, let the buyer tell their boss about this wonderful new product and how it will work within their assortment. Then, you can step right up and give them the song and dance about it.

How to Justify a Price Increase

Although there are large stores with giant buying power, and some like to crusade for lower prices, it's a fact of life that a manufacturer's costs do occasionally go up. Buyers are taught to hate price increases and are very adept at ignoring or delaying them. My best effort pushed a price increase back one year from the date it was delivered to all the other stores. It's part of the game. If a buyer can continue their current cost and retail prices, while their competition is forced to raise their retails, they might get an edge in the marketplace. The other side of the coin is that, if you permit this, you might be violating some of the US laws mentioned in a previous chapter.

So how do you step around this hurdle? Is there a delicate way to deliver a price increase and get it to stick? If the sounds of a salesperson begging won't move the buyer to change the cost prices, perhaps you need a different, more effective, professional strategy.

A samurai salesperson is wise and very detailed. A manufacturer receives price increases from their suppliers, especially when the cost of raw materials goes up. Bring copies of those documents, on the letterhead of *your* suppliers, with you to the buyer's office. Explain what is happening to these raw materials on the world market and how it is impacting your business. When your factory is being forced to accept higher prices, you are asking for the buyer's support too. Normally, this documentation is satisfactory and most buyers will negotiate a specific date to start paying the new price.

Granted, you can still encounter "bulldozer" or "intimidator" buyers who could care less about your explanations. They're looking to obtain hero status within their corporations and battling your price increases, and postponing them, is akin to slaying the fire-breathing dragon in mythology. If your corporation critically needs to raise prices, you will require the backing of your customers. When a customer won't cooperate, there are many questions you will need to ask yourself. Did you sufficiently explain the situation to the buyer? Are they fighting you because of their corporate policies? Are you asking at the wrong time, or are business conditions unsuitable for raising prices? Do you need to get your management involved in the discussion?

When all else fails, maybe you need to ask the buyer very directly why they're opposing you. In this case, positive confrontation is called for.

Should You Load a Price to Cover Coop/Rebate/Returns/Discounts or Go Net-Net?

A load is defined as increasing a cost price by including additional financial incentives. For example, if your base cost for manufacturing an item is $1.00 and your profit structure needs to sell it at $2.00 (a 50% profit on every sale), you would have to build (add) other programs into your price. If a retail store requires a 5% coop allowance, 2% for rebates, and 1% for paying the invoice quickly, you'd need to add or load 8% more into your cost invoice price. In this instance, your cost price would need to be $2.16 for this item. Therefore, you are making your $1 profit and have extra funds accumulating (accruing) to cover the buyer's advertising, rebate and quick pay discount.

Let's suppose that you didn't build these incentives into your price, but agreed to pay them to the buyer. Those funds would be deducted out of your profit. Would you really want to do that? Although buyers won't admit it, most of them understand that financial incentives are part of their invoice cost.

If you're dealing with a buyer and a store that demands a "net-net" price, they're asking for you to sell it to them without any financial packages added. These stores have internal advertising budgets and don't want to raise cost prices to bankroll ad dollars.

You must be extremely careful in all situations where you are first establishing a relationship with a store or buyer. Even if the buyer says that they want a "net-net," "down and dirty" price, are you positive that they won't bill you for advertising or other incentives in the future? Most of the retailers that employed me required vendor incentive programs and billed the manufacturer for coop advertising, as well as earned rebates. I have witnessed novice salespeople who agreed to a net price, only to find that the buyer expected them to pay for additional incentives later on. You must ask the hard questions up front in a relationship and put it all into writing— "we're selling to you at this price, which doesn't include advertising, rebates, etc." Don't verbally agree to a net price. What will happen to you when there is a buyer change and amnesia strikes the retailer? Guess who's pocket will be dipped into to fund the coop and rebate?

The answer to the question—should you load a price—is yes, if you're dealing with a store that typically has that type of relationship with their suppliers. Ask other manufacturers how they deal with a retailer or buyer and plan accordingly.

THOUGHT #15

Chinese proverb: Customers are treasure; goods are but straw.

Products are continuously created, but you must always keep your focus on the customer. Are you satisfying your immediate customer, the retail buyer and store, as well as the end user? Keep the customer happy. You'll want to keep repeating the above proverb when you have to face the next topic.

Dirty tricks

I wish the world was highly ethical and everyone offered great communication coupled with positive dispositions. Unfortunately, that isn't the case. Retailing is part of the business world and there are times when hidden agendas are utilized, or games are being played. I've seen dirty tricks disappear when a relationship has grown over many years or has graduated to a strategic alliance. However, great relationships don't guarantee that underhanded methods aren't being employed. Samurai salespeople have to remain vigilant in all situations.

Disclaimer: *I want to emphasize that most retailers and buyers are highly ethical professionals and wouldn't engage in surreptitious strategies. They have built their careers and stores based on higher standards of behavior. However, you might occasionally encounter the more furtive elements of retailing. As a public service, I'm offering a few of the better ploys I've heard about over the years.*

1) **Good cop, bad cop.** You've seen this technique on all the police shows. The suspect is brought into an interrogation room, and the bad cop is hammering away on the felon's head. Suddenly, the door opens and the good cop enters, admonishing the bad cop. The bad cop leaves the room and the good cop calmly talks with the suspect, offering him a drink or a cigarette. The criminal appreciates the good cop's approach and tells the good cop every secret imaginable. Have you ever played this game with a retailer? Some of them have perfected this approach and it has become an art form. Many plan this attack and see if they can suck you into the action. Normally, it will be the senior manager from the retail store that is pummeling you, and the buyer becomes the good cop, saving the day and the relationship. "Our president is really upset with your offer," a buyer could tell you, "but if you give me this (fill in the blank), he'll be satisfied and leave us alone." The insinuation can be that senior management will totally muck up the works or that the entire relationship is sliding into a chasm. Regardless, there is an implied threat. Occasionally, the roles will reverse and the member of senior management will become the good cop, pulling the rabid and unfeeling buyer off the traumatized back of an unprotected vendor.

2) **Playing one vendor against another.** Many manufacturers have complained to me about this practice. Even long standing relationships can be subjected to this technique. Normally, you receive a phone call telling you about competitive action in the marketplace that directly impacts your business. Your competition has scheduled a direct attack on you, dropping prices and making all kinds of offers to the retailer in an attempt to capture your business. They've effectively made you appear to be overcharging the buyer for similar or identical merchandise, and that makes the buyer feel like a weak negotiator. Now, the buyer is on the telephone and wants to know how you are going to handle this problem. If it's a significant price drop, you've got a lot of thinking to do: shall you keep your turf and match prices, come close to the competitive bid, or take a tough line, preferring not to change. Aggressive vendors will fight back, unwilling to lose market share. Many folks will cut their prices slightly. The buyers have nothing to lose in this scenario; regardless of what happens, they gain profitability. It's preferred that the existing vendor, whom I call the vendor of record, cut prices and the

merchandise on the shelves remains unchanged. The buyers really aren't looking for a vendor switch, just a price improvement; switching vendors puts old and new inventory (different looking packages) on the shelves, or requires markdowns or merchandise returns. All of that can be messy, labor intensive and time consuming. Now, be aware that playing one vendor against another can occur several ways: 1) there really is a competitive offer that came in unsolicited; 2) the buyer encouraged another vendor to bring in a bid because the buyer isn't happy with your performance; 3) the buyer is under severe profit pressure and can only achieve their goals with a dramatic improvement via a price drop; or, 4) there is no competitive bid, and the buyer is lying to you. It has been my experience that the first scenario is the most common; there often is an actual competitive proposal that came in without the buyer's help. However, you do need to be aware that the other possibilities do occur. If the buyer isn't happy with your performance, what is wrong and why weren't you on top of the problem? The correct response to all of them is to alter your pricing, or provide some other form of benefit to the retailer. If you choose to play hardball with the buyer, disbelieving that any harm will come to you, you are inviting some very bad luck. Heavy price negotiations often involve the buyer's superiors. If you don't give the buyer a positive response, they will lose face with their management. How many buyers will tolerate that for too long?

3) **Incremental.** Here's a word that strikes fear into the hearts of many suppliers. Retailers expect to make incremental gains every year—in sales and profit increases. Buyers are rated on how much they can increase their advertising allowances, rebates and the ability to get better pricing from you. You can anticipate getting pounded on "incremental" issues every year; the buyers are paid to do so. Can you improve your rebate program if the retailer achieves significantly higher levels of purchasing? Isn't it worth your while to invest more money into advertising if the buyer is focusing heavily on your merchandise, pushing the goods at retail? Aggressive vendors find ways to keep pushing the envelope on this one, without raising their prices. Are there greater cost efficiencies that the factory achieves when more merchandise is being pumped through the machinery? If so, can you pass those savings on to your premiere customers?

4) **Threats.** Into all lives, a few threats must appear. There are the perennial favorite—competitive threats—which will never completely go away. Hey, you live in a capitalist country, with a competitive market. There are also "buyer threats," typically found from the bulldozing, intimidating buyers. You can often run into mild-mannered threats posed by other buyer-types. It is part of the landscape and you should be prepared for them. Most threats need to have a counter reaction; ignoring them will insure a spot for you on the vendor wall of shame. Buyers hate salespeople who ignore them—especially people who ignore their threats. It's a sign of weakness or ineptitude. Regardless of who is threatening you or the nature of the threat, you must prepare for this eventuality and have strategies in place. It's all right to feign surprise to the buyer when the threat occurs, but you'd better have an action plan established in your cranium. If a threat sends a manufacturer into a tailspin, the buyer is going to re-evaluate your ability to remain a viable vendor.

5) **Bait and switch advertising.** Unless you'd like to tango with the Federal Trade Commission (FTC), you need to stay as far away as possible from bait and switch schemes. The FTC defines bait and switch as advertising that "...is an alluring but insincere offer to sell a product or service which the advertiser in truth does not intend or want to sell. Its purpose is to switch consumers from buying the advertised merchandise, in order to sell something else, usually at a higher price or on a basis more advantageous to the advertiser." An ad shouldn't run if it contains an offer to sell a product "... when the offer is not a bona fide effort to sell the advertised product." If your buyer is using your merchandise to lure people into their store, but has insufficient quantities on hand, that could be perceived negatively by the authorities, and would infuriate the consumer. If store sales associates are encouraging customers not to purchase an advertised item but are, instead, referring them to a different product, that won't thrill consumer advocates and the federal government either. Most retailers are extremely watchful for this type of behavior today and they don't want to suffer the consequences. However, you need to be aware of the practice.

6) **Famous maker and hide the salami.** These cute advertising tricks are deceptive and often have vendor's blessings. "Famous maker" is utilized in advertising when a product is being sold at a price that would agitate the manufacturer of the goods. Even though vendors can't dictate retail prices to retailers, if a

123

product is blasted out at or below cost, the supplier will get a slew of nasty phone calls from all their other affected customers. Seeking to avoid the carnage, clever buyers will hide the identity of the merchandise, but alert the consumer that they would recognize the famous brand. "Hide the salami" was a phrase I heard along the way, referring to a regular practice of hiding the manufacturer's name in print ads. If merchandise is mediocre and didn't have a "famous maker," some slick retail buyers often would hide the identity, pretending it was great quality. Hide the salami is intended to be more misleading than famous maker. Regardless, you need to watch how your buyer describes your goods on ad.

7) **Other dirty tricks.** There should be specific names for some of the more bizarre tactics used by buyers. The most heinous act I've heard about involved a retail buyer who had run out of ad monies with a vendor. The buyer was "hung" with a substantial amount of that supplier's inventory. Clearly, the buyer had overbought and had miscalculated the quantity of merchandise necessary. Exhausting all options, including a frank discussion about the situation, the buyer was encouraged by the divisional merchandise manager (not me) to buy even more product from this supplier. They would run another ad with a dramatic savings message—save 50%. Since all goods purchased from this supplier had advertised funding built into the prices, the buyer computed how many additional items to purchase to generate enough money to pay for a newspaper ad. The divisional merchandise manager and buyer knew that they'd never sell through the additional inventory, but they didn't care. The new purchase from the vendor would never be put out on the sales floor. Instead, it would be carefully stored in the warehouse. It was a purchase designed only to accrue ad funds, which would be immediately spent to move out the original overstocked goods. Are you following this action? Pretty unethical, right? Nope. It gets much better. After the ad ran, the plan was for the buyer to instantly take the goods sitting in the warehouse and ship them back to the supplier—without a return authorization. An additional advertisement had been funded, the overstock was to be liquidated, and the new shipment would go back to the supplier. Yes, a "wonderful" plan if you're a miscreant. This story did have a happy ending, nonetheless. The supplier quickly figured out what was going on after receiving truckloads of goods in January, approximately one month after

having shipped the identical merchandise to the retailer. The buyer and the divisional merchandise manager were caught and had to negotiate an alternative way out of the problem—extended payment dating from the supplier, and the buyer eating a bunch of markdowns. I think they've sold through the merchandise by now.

Chapter 16
Doors, Paths, Wisdom, Success

THOUGHT #16

Thinking unhurriedly, understanding that it is the duty of warriors to practice this science, determine that today you will overcome your self of the day before, tomorrow you will win over those of lesser skill, and later you will win over those of greater skill. Practicing in accord with this book, you should determine not to let your mind get sidetracked. .... This is something that requires thorough examination, with a thousand days of practice for training and ten thousand days of practice for refinement.[13]

Miyamoto Musashi

Musashi was a great warrior and amazing philosopher, and his words are very inspirational when you read them today. Famous warriors, like celebrated salespeople, spend incalculable hours refining their skills, perfecting their talents until all their preparation makes them ready for battle. They do not rest, and they believe that their performance always can be improved through additional training, calculation and practice. The most illustrious names in business, the arts, sports and warfare did not wake up one day with their abilities in place. They learned from other technicians and masters in their fields, they paid attention to details, and then they channeled all this information into a blended mixture, adding a unique approach—they developed their own style and personality.

From the moment you walk out your front door in the morning, you have a choice. You can walk down one path or another. Do you choose to have a splendid day, motivating people with your magnificent attitude, or would you rather grouse your way through your time on this planet? If you want to grow as an individual and become a samurai salesperson, you have a choice to make. One path will take you to excellence, experience, knowledge, training and numerous rewards; one path will lead you to mediocrity or misery. The distance down both roads can be long. Successful people will tell you that their trip hasn't been easy, and that they have worked diligently to stay on course.

Is it your destiny to be a samurai salesperson? It can be. Destiny can be altered and, like clay, molded into any shape you desire. I firmly believe that and so should you. What door do you want to open? What path would you prefer to traverse? Will you walk towards enlightenment or spend your entire existence befuddled, mired in a substandard career, never achieving your full potential? Can you attain success or will you chase after the specter of success for your lifetime? We have choices.

I started my business career over 25 years ago and, in the beginning, I traveled a meandering course, filled with landmines and detours. My approach was disorganized at best. When logic and wisdom weren't available, rather than striving for excellence and learning new ways to deal with situations, I waved a figurative sword fiercely over my head, threatening any salesperson who would dare to approach me. My path led to darkness, despair and treachery. Fortunately for me, and those around me, I ultimately discovered a happier and more productive direction for my life.

Remember the story at the beginning of this book, in Chapter 1, when I crushed a salesperson and he appeared to be having a stroke in front of me? Although it was a long time ago, I recall it distinctly. That wasn't my proudest moment. Yet, instances like that should make all of us pause, reconsider our direction in life, and draw significant conclusions, aimed at self-improvement. Today, I'm committed to helping people grow as individuals, to expand communication in the business world so that more products are produced and sold, and to help you become more successful in your careers. I'd like to see more merchandise purchased by more buyers and salespeople closing more deals. I hope the thoughts in this book will help you to drive your business forward. We have a choice. Are you maximizing the potential of your sales career and connecting with the thought patterns of your customers, the buyers?

You should think like a merchant, thinking like your customer, or you will be a peddler forever. Retail samurai salespeople spend lots of time preparing, studying and refining their approaches. They have examined the buyer's thought processes, the buyer's environment, and the activity in the buying office and what it takes to be a great vendor. Samurai salespeople have mastered advertising and inventory procedures. They've researched the methods of the best corporations. Samurai salespeople understand the six qualities of the best companies and the ten qualities of the best salespeople, and they've incorporated these actions into their business lives.

I encourage you to take the higher path, the road filled with wisdom, strength, power, knowledge and, ultimately, success. I encourage you to be enlightened. There is great pride achieved by those who walk this way and a deep inner satisfaction.

At the beginning of this book I told you to, "think like a merchant or forever act like a peddler." However, if you have followed this course of study, you are aware of something else.

Think like a retail samurai salesperson and you will never be a peddler.

Look forward to your quest for righteousness and wisdom. I hope that it will bring you prosperity.

I encourage you to be strong, to be wise, and to be a samurai!

Glossary

80/20 items

merchandise that contributes 80% of the retail sales at a store. A best selling item.

80/20 rule

80% of sales come from 20% of the items offered.

ad package

a financial incentive given by the manufacturer to the retailer, helping the store to advertise a manufacturer's products

affinity

items that are purchased during the same transaction. i.e., dog food and a food bowl.

anniversary

comparing the sales results from the current fiscal year Vs. the previous years performance. If sales events are properly "anniversaried," ads in the current fiscal year will generate higher sales than the preceding year.

assortment

the selection of merchandise offered by a retail store.

coop advertising

years ago, this meant cooperative advertising, meaning, ads funded by both the retailer and manufacturer. Today, coop means monies provided by the manufacturer to the retailer so the store can advertise the manufacturer's products.

coop allowances

see coop advertising. Funds provided by the manufacturer to be utilized for advertising their products at a retail store.

dating

the amount of time given to the retailer to pay the manufacturer for goods purchased. Dating on an invoice can include payment within ten days, 30 days or more.

dating—quick pay

when a manufacturer gives a financial incentive to a retailer for paying an invoice for merchandise quickly. For example, 2%10N30 means 2% discount if the invoice is paid within 10 days, or the invoice must be paid in full within 30 days.

departments

a financial area of responsibility that groups like merchandise together. For example, a woman's dress department, or hair care department.

differentiation

anything that makes a retail store different from its competition. This can include different merchandise, signing, prices or packaging.

double truck ad

a printed advertisement spanning two pages, running from a left page and across to the right hand page.

EDLP retailers

acronym for every day low price. EDLP retailers don't run sales because their merchandise is at low prices on a daily basis.

fill rate

the percent of merchandise received from a vendor vs. what the retailer actually requested on a purchase order.

financial package

monies given to the retailer as a reward for doing business with a manufacturer. This can include rebate, coop allowances, and other funds.

forecast	a financial plan or budget, attempting to predict the sales or unit movement of products or expenses.
GMROI	acronym for gross margin return on investment. A ratio that expresses the return on the investment for a retail dollar.
handling expenses	costs incurred by retailers and manufacturers for moving, boxing or transporting merchandise.
hard goods	products offered for sale in a retail store that are made of a more rigid construction than apparel. Any non-apparel items in a retail store.
high low retailers	retailers that sell merchandise at a higher price during non-sale periods, then run goods at lower prices during sale events.
incentive	a financial reward given to a retailer for growing business with a manufacturer.
incentive—volume incentive	a financial reward for increasing purchases with a manufacturer. See rebate.
initial margin percent	difference between the landed cost of a product and its selling price, expressed as a percentage.
inventory turn	the number of times that the retailer sells their inventory during the course of a year.
IS	an acronym for Information Systems. Typically, IS is a department within businesses and stores sales information in huge databases.

key item
a best selling product, highly requested by customers.

lift
a sales dollar or unit increase on merchandise resulting from an advertisement or sale event. This is either expressed as dollars or percent lift.

line extension
a new product that is created by a manufacturer that is similar to existing items they offer for sale. However, this product will have other unique characteristics. A vendor offering inexpensive cordless phones might produce a "line extension" with expanded features and benefits.

list price
a suggested retail price that is created by the manufacturer.

load—loading a price
Increasing a cost price by including additional financial incentives. If a retail store required a 5% coop allowance, 2% for rebates, a vendor might increase their cost price by a 7% load.

local market
a geographical area. Chicago is a large market, comprised of many towns or local markets. Each local market can have unique demographics with special ethnic, religious, or age concentrations.

markdown allowances
funds provided by the manufacturer to reimburse the retailer when they lower a retail price.

markdown money
see markdown allowance

mass market retailers
typically defined as large, national retailers that cater to broad demographics. Examples include:

Target, Walmart and Kmart.

merchandise information systems
computerized databases that detail sales information. Same as sales information systems.

net-net
when merchandise is purchased without any financial incentives—advertising, rebate, etc.—included in the price.

open to buy
a financial budget that manages inventory.

planogram
a detailed method for displaying merchandise on a retailer's selling floor. Planograms are printed "road maps" that tell the store associate where to specifically place the products.

point of purchase (POP)
a sign designed to be placed adjacent to merchandise on the sales floor, drawing attention to the product, and providing product features/benefits and price.

profit dollars
the monetary profit on a retail sale that is above the cost purchase price.

profit margin
the percent of each retail sales dollar that is above the cost purchase price. For example, a $50 retail item, that cost $25 to purchase, generates a 50% profit ($25).

rebate
a financial incentive given to the retailer from the manufacturer, returning a percentage of cost purchases back to the retailer in the form of a check. Typically, rebates are connected to purchases hitting specific volume targets with a manufacturer. For example, 1% rebate = purchases of $1 million, 2% rebate = purchases of $2 million, etc.

sales information systems computerized databases that detail sales information. Same as merchandise information systems.

skus an acronym that stands for "stock keeping unit." An sku is a number assigned to an individual product so the retailer can track its sales.

soft goods products offered for sale in a retail store that are apparel.

terms see dating.

top seller see key item

Index

ENDNOTES

[1] Miyamoto Musashi, The Book of Five Rings, trans. Thomas Cleary (Boston: Shambhala Publications, Inc., 1993), p.59

[2] Ibid., p. 16

[3] Miyamoto Musashi, A Book of Five Rings, trans. Victor Harris (Woodstock: The Overlook Press, 2001), p.49

[4] Ibid., p.48

[5] Ibid., p.70

[6] Ibid., p.71

[7] Musashi, trans. Thomas Cleary, op. cit., pp.37-38

[8] Musashi, trans. Thomas Cleary, op. cit., p.38

[9] Musashi, trans. Victor Harris, op. cit., p.75

[10] Musashi, trans. Thomas Cleary, op. cit., p.41

[11] Musashi, trans. Victor Harris, op. cit., pp.86-87

[12] Musashi, trans. Victor Harris, op. cit., p.54

[13] Musashi, trans. Thomas Cleary, op. cit., p.32

ABOUT THE AUTHOR

Merrill Lehrer is an author and speaker, and head samurai merchant at Retail Samurai Sales, a manufacturing, sales and retail consulting firm, based in San Diego, California. Merrill has over twenty-five years retail buying and selling experience, having served as divisional merchandise manager at Petco, general merchandise manager/senior buyer at Office Depot, and senior buyer for several divisions of Federated Department Stores and other specialty chain stores.

He fought his way from the selling floors of retail stores into the buying offices, ultimately managing multi-billion dollar businesses. During his career, Merrill has worked in the consumer electronics, office products, housewares, home furnishings, pet supplies and musical instruments industries, and many more.

An avid writer, Merrill has produced articles for *USA Today* and many other publications. Currently, he is a columnist for *Pet Age* magazine, Kitchenware News, The Music Trades, SHOPTALK (School, Home & Office Products Association magazine), and Pets International.

Merrill lives with his wife and son in San Diego, California.

Merrill Lehrer
Retail Samurai Sales
858-613-0400
MLehrer@san.rr.com